Railway Track Diagrams
Book 5: Southern & TfL
Edited by Myles Munsey

Preface

Quail Track Diagrams have been published since 1988 and provide a reference to Enthusiasts and Industry alike. Originally drawn by cartographer John Yonge of the Quail Map Co and edited by the late Gerald Jacobs, the updating and publication of these titles were taken over by TRACKmaps in 2004. Now a de-facto standard for a wide range of users from train staff and infrastructure managers to railway enthusiasts and modellers, they contain information which may exist elsewhere and in other forms but are unique in making it all available in one easily portable volume.

Mike Bridge, TRACKmaps August 2019

Introduction to this Edition

The track diagrams in this book comprise the Kent, Sussex and Wessex Routes of Network Rail together with HS1, London Underground, Docklands Light Railway, London Trams and a number of private railways and Heritage lines. Also included is Crossrail in view of its near completion and its route under London. The maps are generally up to date as at August 2019.

There has been considerable change in the 11 years since the publication of the 3rd edition. The most significant transformation by far has been that at London Bridge where lines from Charing Cross/Cannon Street through London Bridge to Deptford,New Cross and New Cross Gate have been completely reorganised and a brand new dive-under facility provided at Bermondsey to enhance capacity. In the same area, the East London Line, under construction in 2008, has been completed together with its depot at New Cross Gate and the connecting Silwood lines.

The demand for more network capacity has led to new depots and stabling sidings either completed or under construction and platform extensions have been widespread, particularly in the South Western Railway suburban area where most stationplatforms have been lengthened. There have been additional platforms installed at Redhill and Gatwick Airport, the International platforms at Waterloo have been returned to Suburban use and new layouts have appeared at Gravesend, Rochester (including a new station), Rainham, Faversham and Ramsgate.

A number of signal boxes have been closed and signalling re-controlled to new major centres at Three Bridges and Basingstoke, including control of the Seaford branch which was about to be transferred to Three Bridges ROC as this book closed for press and is shown in its final form. In Kent, the 2011 opening of the East Kent signalling Centre at Gillingham has eliminated several manual signal boxes along the North Kent Coast to Ramsgate.

There has been some re-organisation of maps in this 4th Edition, the Index is slightly extended, the ELR index has been retained and an LOR index added.

Acknowledgements

The Editor is indebted to Network Rail and its staff for access to industry documents. Several other people have contributed greatly to the compilation of this publication. The significant input of Richard Atkinson, Martyn Brailsford, Mike Bridge, Tim Wild, Stuart Hendry and Ross Muggeridge is both appreciated and recognised.

Other helpful input has been received from Malcolm Jones (Kent & East Sussex Railway), Carl Watson (Arlington Fleet Services, Eastleigh), Phil Lucas and Stuart Strong (Volks Electric Railway), Simon Jennings, Nigel Farebrother, Nik Anthony, Lottie Ramsden, Mick Donovan, John Lacy, Kev Adlam, Alan Green and Pat Bell.

Acknowledgement is also due to Phil Deaves from whose website a tremendous amount of ELR and LOR related data has been a constant reference, to Peter Scott (the editor of Minor Railways) and to the Branch Line Society.

The Editor and Publisher would also like to especially thank cartographers Dave Padgett and Leanne Kelman who have quietly dealt with the changes to layouts and wholesale redraws of large sections that have arisen.

Myles Munsey

1st Edition 1994
2nd Edition 2002
3rd Edition 2008 (reprinted 2011, 2012, 2014, 2017)
4th Edition 2019

Published by TRACKmaps, PO Box 5259, Beckington, Frome, BA11 9DD. Website: www.trackmaps.co.uk

Edited by Myles Munsey

Cartography by Dave Padgett & Leanne Kelman
Typesetting by Leanne Kelman

Printed by Brightsea Print Group, Clyst Honiton EX5 2UL
Cover design by Jan McFarlane at ArtWebCo, Swindon SN2 8YY
Cover photography, see opposite

Publisher's Note
Every effort has been made by the Editor to ensure the accuracy of the information in the book is as correct as possible at the time of going to press. Notwithstanding, the Publishers welcome corrections, updates or suggestions for application to future editions. Contributions are preferred through the Contact Us page on the website or by post to the address above.

KEY

————	Running Line	*86.34* *(Not italic* *if Station* *mileage)*	Distance in Miles and chains from specified zero 1 Mile = 1760 yards / 1.6km 80 chains = 1 Mile 1 chain = 22 yards / 20.11m
————	Siding		
————	Electrified overhead (25kV AC unless stated)	*57.600*	Distance in Kilometres
————	Electrified 3rd rail (750V DC)	I 93	Whole mileposts, shown on the appropriate side of the line
————	Electrified 4th rail (LUL) (630V DC)	I *32*	Whole kilometre posts
————	Electrified, overhead & Conductor rail	*81.30̅|*	End of mileage run
··············	Proposed or under construction.	*113.76* ———— **COM** *105.70*	Lineside mileage change
——●——	Line obstructed	BML 1	ELR-Engineer's Line Reference (Prefix and suffix numbers indicate sub-divisions and their boundaries)
——○---	Line 'in situ' but out of use, partly dismantled, buried, or overgrown	[SO 130]	Line of Route Code
——•——	Change of Signalling mandate	**3**	Platform with number (May be supplemented by sub-divisions. e.g. (a), (b), (c), 'N' or North etc)
WX ‖ WR	Network Rail Territory boundary	⑦	Indicates number of carriages per platform (approx 20m lengths)
(TLW) | (TEB)	Signal control limits (Within an area, plates on automatic signals may reflect actual line description)	⋮	Proposed platform
⟋ ⟍❖⟋	Diamond Crossing / Switch Diamond	▭	Former Royal Mail platform
—)---(—	Tunnel	▭	Platform out of use
≃	Viaduct or Bridge under Rail	⌂	Other feature (labelled)
—I—	Selected Motorway / Trunk Road bridges over rail	▨	Loading bank / dock
—+—	Network Rail operated level crossing	*East Kent SC* *(EK)(EV)(NK)* ⊠	ASC, IECC, SB, SC, SCC or ROC with code (underlined text relates)
—I—	User-worked crossing with Telephone	▨	Control Panel
←——→	Track signalled in both directions (a double arrow indicates normal direction of travel)	◪	Gate Box
—⋈—	Private siding boundary, or gate	□ ⊙	Ground Frame GF / Ground Switch Panel GSP or Shunting Frame SF. ⓢ Indicates 'Shut in' facility
⌐——	Sand Drag / Trap Point	✵	Radio electronic token block / Token exchange point
—◯—	Turntable / Friction Arrester, Buffer or other stop	¶	Proposed closure
—‖—	Gantry Rails (Freightliner Terminal)	O	Water tower
—x—x—x—	Fence	∧	Summit, height in feet
∧∧∧∧∧∧∧	Wall / Bank / Cliff	*(Alderbury Jn)* ●	Indicates a former Jn, Station or Signal Box
———▲———	Hot Axle Box Detector (HABD), Wheel Impact Load Detector (WILD) or Wheelchex Device		

Guide references are given to pre-nationalisation, pre-grouping and sometimes pioneer railways e.g. S:LCD

GENERAL ABBREVIATIONS

AA	Acid Application	ft	Feet	Qy	Query concerning distances etc, unresolved
ABP	Associated British Ports	GC	Gantry Crane	REC	Reception
AC	Alternating Current	GDS	Goods	RETB	Radio Electronic Token Block
ARR	Arrival	GL	Goods Loop	REV	Reversing or Reversible line
ASC	Area Signalling Centre	GS	Goods Shed	ROC	Rail Operating Centre
bdy	boundary	H	Headshunt	RR	Run-Round
BCH	Branch	HABD	Hot Axle Box Detector	S	South
BR	British Rail	HH	Hopper House	S & T	Signal & Telegraph
CET	Controlled Emission Toilet Discharge	HL	High Level	SB	Signal Box or Southbound
CL	Crossing Loop on Single Line	HST	High Speed Train	SC	Signalling Centre
COM	Change of Mileage	IECC	Integrated Electronic Control Centre	SCC	Signalling (or Service) Control Centre
CR	Cripple Siding	IET	Intercity Express Train	Sdg(s)	Siding(s)
CW	Carriage Washer	Jn	Junction	SD	Sand Drag
C&W	Carriage & Wagon	Jt	Joint	SF	Shunting Frame
D	Connections Disconnected	km	kilometres	SIMBIDS	Simplified Bi-Directional Signalling
DA	Down Avoiding	LC	Level Crossing (manned, automatic or open)	SN	Shunt Neck
DC	Direct Current	LHS	Locomotive Holding Siding	SP	Switch Panel
DE	Down Electric	LL	Low Level	SS	Shunt Spur
DED	Diesel Electric Depot	loe	limit of electrification	TA	Tamper Siding
DEP	Departure	LP	Loop	TB	Turnback Siding
DF	Down Fast	LPG	Liquified petroleum gas	TEP	Token Exchange Point
DG	Down Goods	LS	Locomotive Shed	TL	Traffic Lights
DGL	Down Goods Loop	LW	Locomotive Washer	TMD	Traction Maintenance Depot
DL	Down Loop	M	Middle	T&RSMD	Traction & Rolling Stock Maintenance Depot
DM	Down Main	m ch	Miles and Chains	U&D	Up & Down
DMD	Diesel Maintenance Depot	M&EE	Mechanical & Electrical Engineer	UA	Up Avoiding
DMUD	Diesel Multiple Unit Depot	MGR	'Merry-go-round'	UE	Up Electric
DN	Down	MN	Main	UF	Up Fast
DPL	Down Passenger Loop	MOD	Ministry of Defence	UFC	Underframe Cleaning
DR	Down Relief	MU	Maintenance Unit	UFN	Until Further Notice
DRS	Down Refuge Sidings	N	North	UG	Up Goods
DS	Down Slow or Down Siding	NB	Northbound	UGL	Up Goods Loop
DSB	Down Suburban	Ng	Narrow gauge	UH	Unloading Hopper
DT	Down Through	NIRU	Not in regular use	UL	Up Loop
E	East	NR	Network Rail	UM	Up Main
EB	Eastbound	NT	No Telephone provided (on LC)	UPL	Up Passenger Loop
EGF	Emergency Ground Frame	OHC	Overhead Crane	UR	Up Relief
EMD	Electric Maintenance Depot	OHLE	Overhead Line Equipment	URS	Up Refuge Siding
EMUD	Electric Multiple Unit Depot	ONS	Overhead Neutral Section	US	Up Slow
Engrs	Engineers' Sidings	OOU	Out of Use	USB	Up Suburban
eol	End of Line	OTM	On-track Maintenance	UT	Up Through
ERTMS	European Rail Traffic Management System	P	Points padlocked	V or Vdct	Viaduct
ESP	Emergency Signalling Panel	PAD	Prefabricated Assembly Depot	W	West
ETCS	European Train Control System	PL	Passenger Loop	WB	Westbound or Weighbridge
FA	Flushing Apron	PSB	Power Signal Box	WD	War Department or Wheelchex Device
FP	Fuelling Point or Footpath	PW	Permanent Way	WILD	Wheel Impact Load Detector
				WL	Wheel Lathe
				yds	yards

SUPPLEMENTARY ABBREVIATIONS FOR THIS BOOK

AR	Network Rail Anglia Route	LSW	former London and South Western Railway
CCOS	Crossrail Central Operating Section	LTrams	London Trams
CTRL	Channel Tunnel Rail Link (HS1)	LU	London Underground
DNS	Former Didcot, Newbury and Southampton Railway	MSW	former Midland and South Western Jn Railway
DSDA	Defence Storage and Distribution Agency	N&SWJn	former North and South Western Jn Railway
EM	Network Rail East Midlands Route	RFF	Réseau Ferré de France
ET	Eurotunnel	RfL	Rail for London
GC	former Great Central Railway	S	former Southern Railway
GE	former Great Eastern Railway	S&DJR	Former Somerset and Dorset Joint Railway
GN	former Great Northern Railway	SE	former South Eastern Railway
GTR	Govia Thameslink Railway	SER	South Eastern Railway
GW	former Great Western Railway	SNCF	Société Nationale des Chemins de Fer Français
KT	Network Rail Kent Route	SO	Southern Region
LBSC	former London, Brighton and South Coast Railway	SR	Southern (part of GTR)
LCD	former London, Chatham and Dover Railway	SWR	South Western Railway (former Southwest Trains)
LGV	Ligne à Grande Vitesse (High Speed Line)	SX	Network Rail Sussex Route
LMS	former London Midland and Scottish Railway	TfL	Transport for London
LNE	former London and North Eastern Railway	TGV	Train à Grande Vitessse (High Speed Train)
LNE	Network Rail London North East Route	WL	former West London Joint Railway
LNW	former London and North Western Railway	WLE	former West London Extension Joint Railway
LNW	Network Rail London North West Route	WR	Network Rail Western Route
LPTB	former London Passenger Transport Board	WX	Network Rail Wessex Route

LEVEL CROSSING ABBREVIATIONS

Abbreviation	Description	Abbreviation	Description
(ABCL) *	Automatic Barrier Crossing, locally monitored	(OC)/(OPEN)	Open Crossing (non-automatic), without barriers or gates
(AHBC) *	Automatic Half-Barrier Crossing, monitored by signaller	(RC)	Remotely Controlled crossing with barriers
(AOCL) *	Automatic Open Crossing, locally monitored	(OMSL)	Automatic Crossing with overlay Miniature Stop Lights (train controlled)
(AOCL+B)	Automatic Open Crossing (half barriers), locally monitored	(TMO)	Traincrew Operated crossing
(AOCR)	Automatic Open Crossing, remotely monitored	(TMOB)	Traincrew Operated Barrier
(BW)	Bridle Way (only shown if telephone provided)	(TMOG)	Traincrew Operated Gates
(CCTV)	MCB Crossing, remotely monitored by signaller using Closed Circuit Television	(UWC)	User-Worked accommodation or occupation crossing, with telephone to contact signaller
(FP)	Footpath crossing (generally shown if telephone provided)		
(MCB)	Manually controlled Crossing with Barriers	(UWC-UI)	User-Worked accommodation or occupation crossing, with telephone to contact signaller and with additional user information
(MCB-OD)	MCB with Obstruction Detection		
(MCG)	Manually controlled Crossing with Gates	(UW~)	User-Worked crossing where ~ represents (B) Barriers
(MGH)	Manually operated Crossing, hand worked		(G) Gates Barriers (K) Kissing gates or (W) Wickets
(MGW)	Manually controlled Crossing with Wickets	(WL)	Barrow or Foot Crossing with White Light Indicators
(MSL) *	Automatic Crossing with Miniature Stop Lights (includes earlier designations R/G, MSL and MWL)		

* (-X) shown after these abbreviations (e.g. AHBC-X) indicates that the crossing works automatically for movements in the wrong direction.

In some cases, the code of the controlling signal box may be shown, e.g. Cresswell (AHBC)(CL).

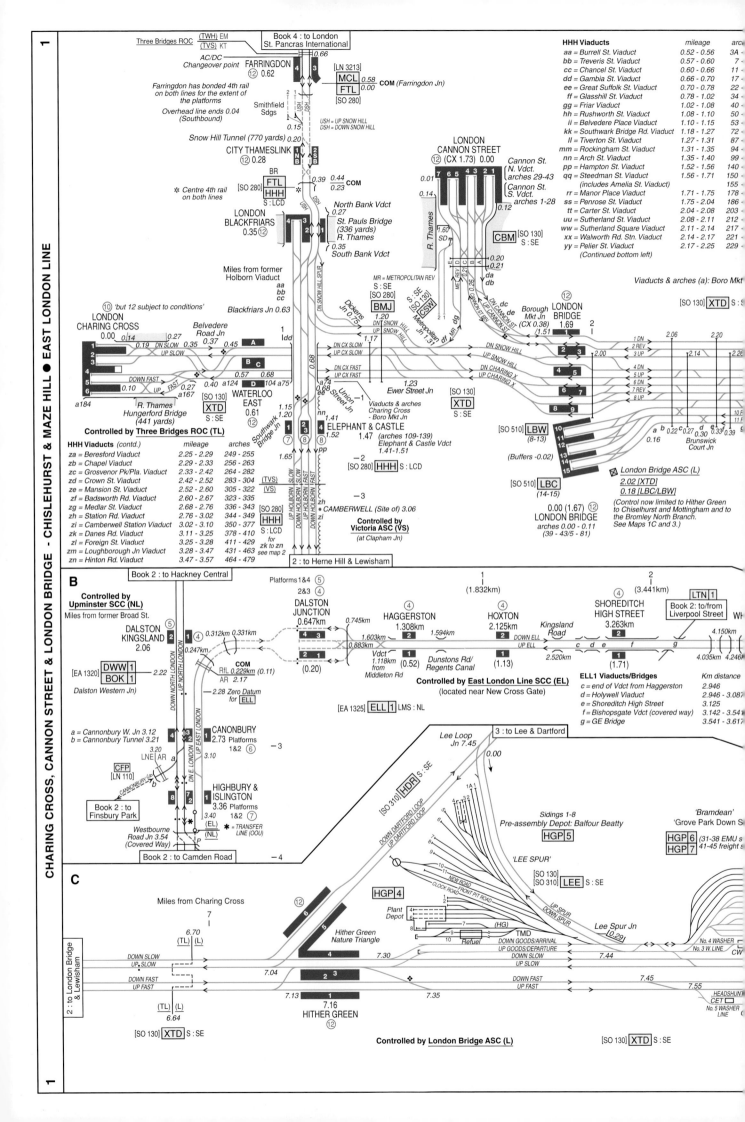

LBC & LBW Viaducts	mileage	LBC arches	LBW arches
a = St. Thomas St. Viaduct	0.04 - 0.19	various	various
b = (Unamed)	0.19 - 0.20	1, 2	various
c = Brunswick Viaduct	0.20 - 0.23	3 - 6	859 - 856
d = Roper Lane Viaduct	0.23 - 0.30	7A - 17C	854 - 839
e = Bacons Viaduct	0.32 - 0.35	22 - 28C	833 - 826
f = Tanner Viaduct	0.35 - 0.38	30 - 33C	825 - 811
g = Maltby Viaduct	0.38 - 0.45	34A - 54C	809 - 788
h = Marquis of Wellington Viaduct	0.45 - 0.50	55A - 66B	785 - 775
i = Perseverance Viaduct	0.50 - 0.53	67C - 71B	773 - 763
k = Bevingtons Viaduct	0.53 - 0.67	72A - 105C	760A - 724
l = Enid St. Viaduct	0.67 - 0.69	106A - 110B	722 - 713
m = Dockley Rd. Viaduct	0.69 - 0.74	111A - 120	708 - 700
n = Lucey Rd. Viaduct	0.74 - 1.01	123 - 140	697 - 680
o = Clement's Viaduct	1.05 - 1.08	144 - 160B	676 - 661
q = Blue Anchor Viaduct	1.08 - 1.28	161C - 215C	654 - 596
r = Almond Rd. Arches	1.28 - 1.48	1A - 45	1.28 - 1.60
s = Rotherhithe Rd. Arches	1.49 - 1.59	46 - 54	592 - 500
t = Jarrow Rd. Arches	1.61 - 1.66	1 - 14	1.60 - 1.62
			500A - 500L

CBM Viaducts	mileage	arches
da = Crown Wharf Viaduct	0.20 - 0.21	235 - 233
db = Park St. Viaducts North	0.21 - 0.27	232 - 205
dc = Winchester Viaduct	0.27 - 0.29	203 - 201
de = Borough Market Viaduct	0.29 - 0.33	

CSW Viaducts	mileage	arches
df = Redcross Viaduct	1.37 - 1.41	185 - 190
dg = Park St. Viaducts South	1.41 - 1.46	192 - 199

NKL Viaducts	mileage	arches
na = Childers St. Viaduct	4.24 - 4.26	328 - 321
nb = Etta St. Viaduct	4.26 - 4.34	295 - 282
nc = Dorking Rd. Viaduct	4.34 - 4.45	278 - 246
nd = Kerry Rd. Viaduct	4.45 - 4.57	243 - 208
ne = Edward Place Viaduct	4.57 - 4.60	206 - 200
nf = Payne St. Viaduct	4.60 - 4.66	197 - 179
ng = Ffinch St. Viaduct	4.66 - 4.76	177 - 130
nh = Mechanics Path Viaduct	4.76 - 5.08	128 - 97
ni = Browne House Viaduct	5.08 - 5.11	95 - 87
nj = Farrer House Viaduct	5.11 - 5.15	85 - 76
nk = Sun Wharf Viaduct	5.15 - 5.20	74 - 60
nl = Harts Wharf Viaduct	5.20 - 5.26	57 - 45
nm = Brewery Viaduct	5.26 - 5.28	42 - 35

Viaducts and arches east of London Bridge
ELR routes XTD, LBW, LBC

Routes XTD & LBW share the arches of the
former London & Greenwich Rly. to arch 593
From arch 593 (XTD 3.17, LBC & LBW 1m 28ch)
the LBC route separates
From arch 500 (XTD 3m 48ch, LBW 1m 60ch)
the LBW route separates
From arch 470 (XTD 3m 54ch) the New Cross
Spur separates

Controlled by Three Bridges ROC (TL)
Miles from Charing Cross

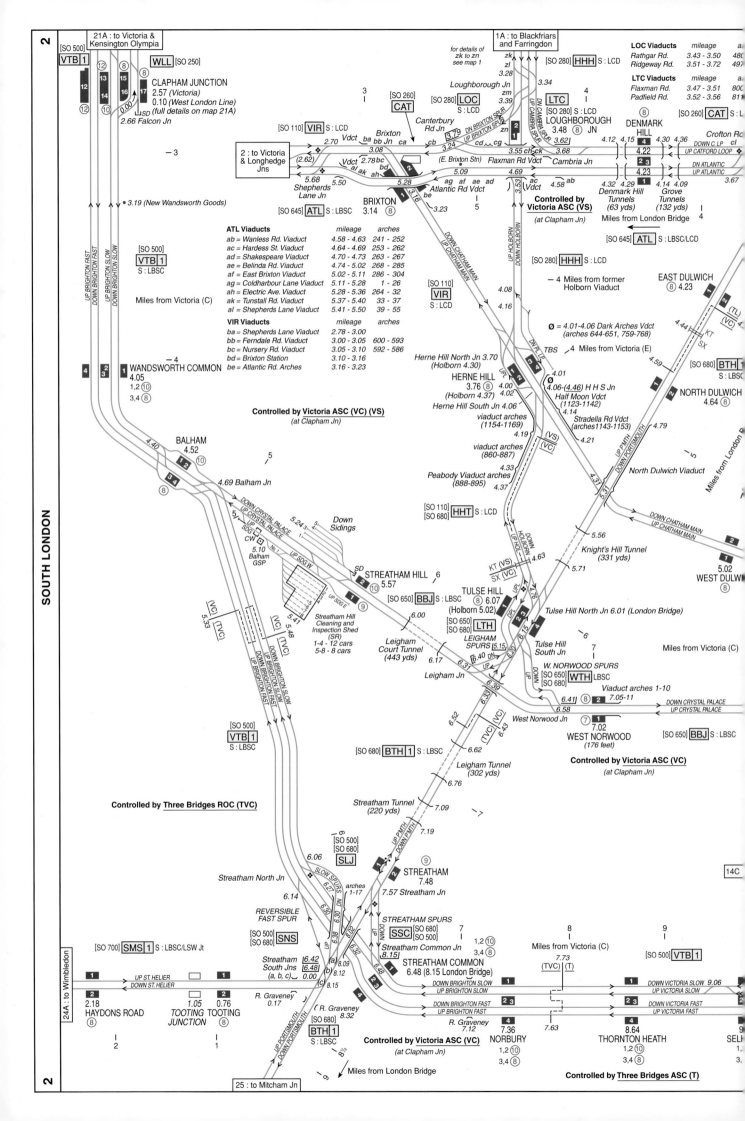

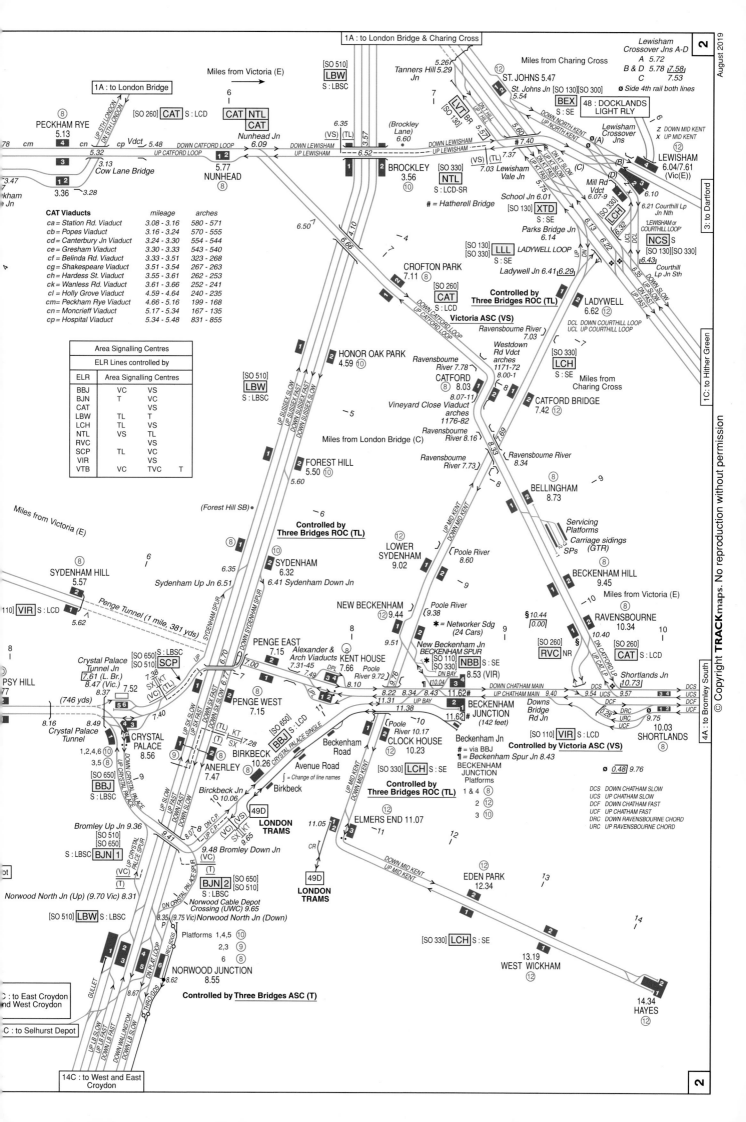

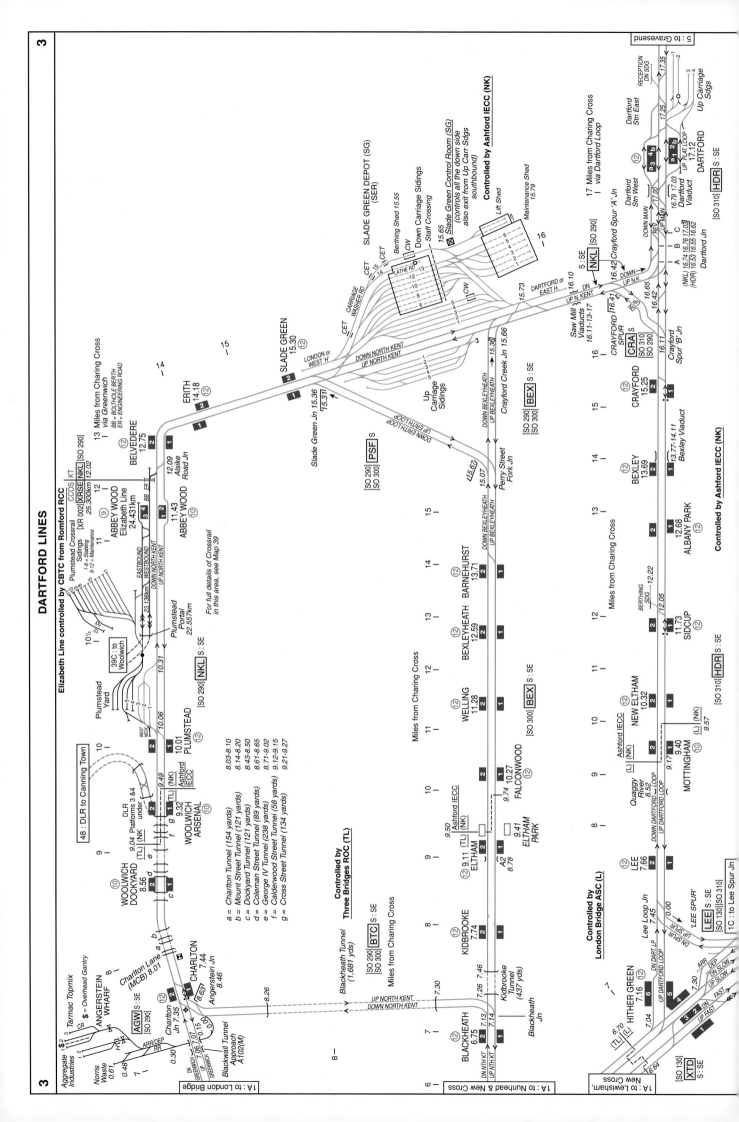

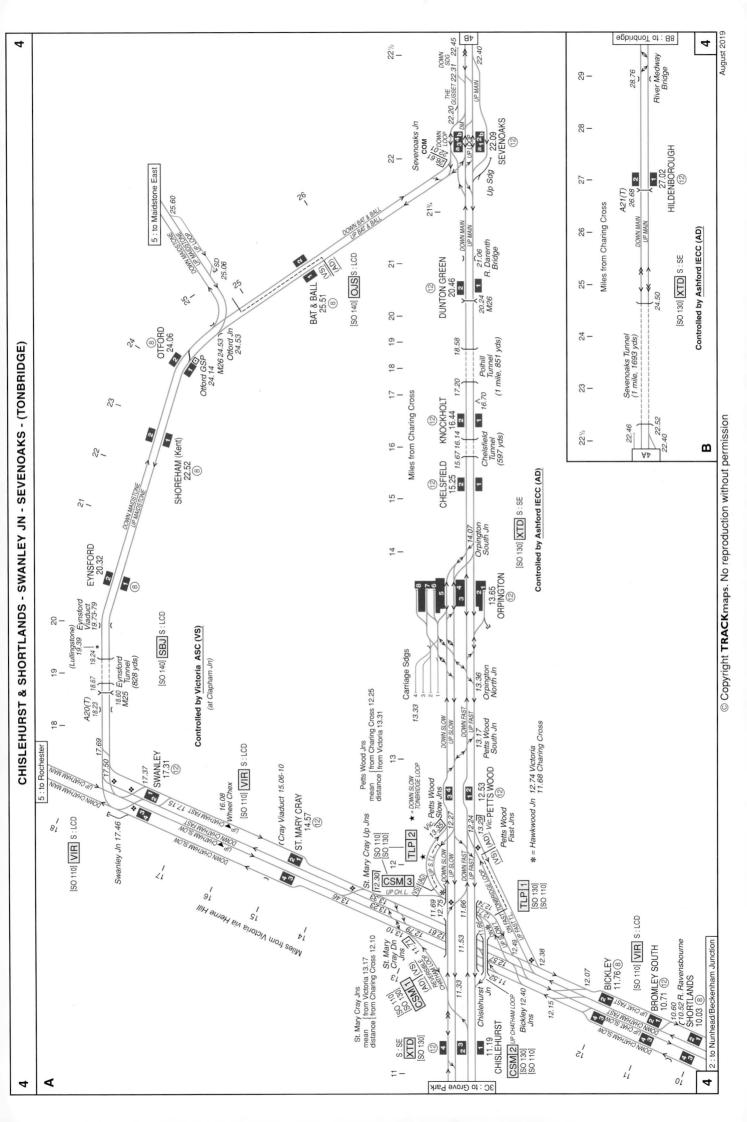

August 2019

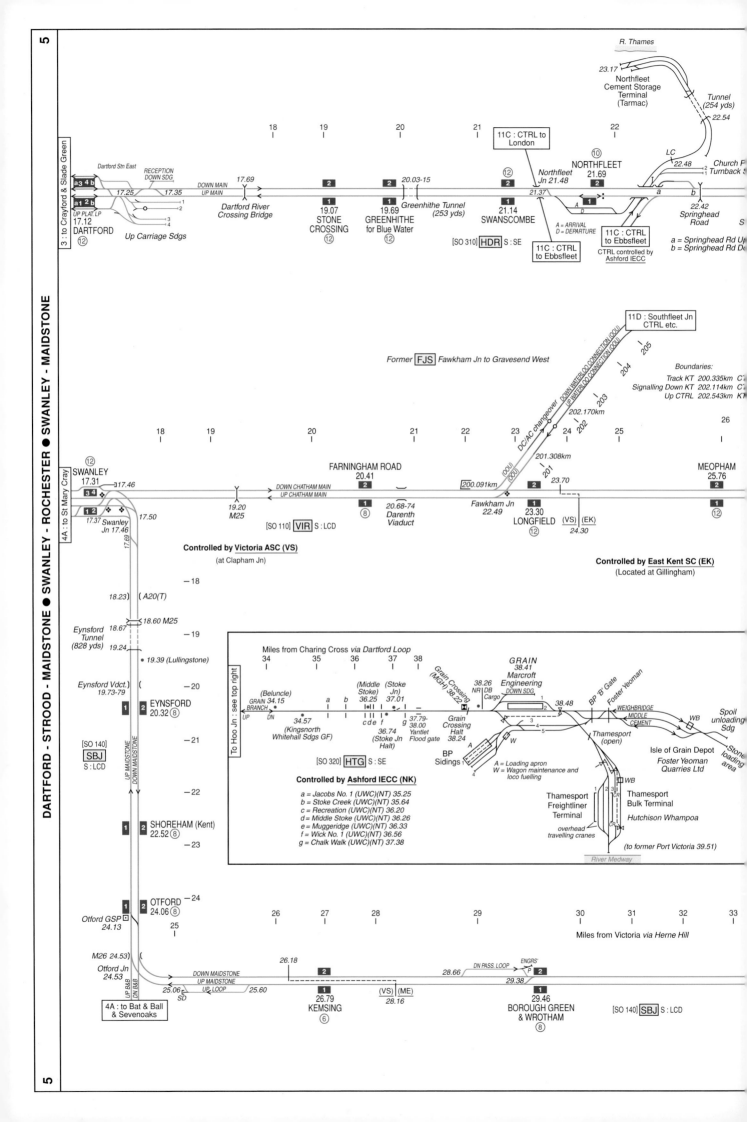

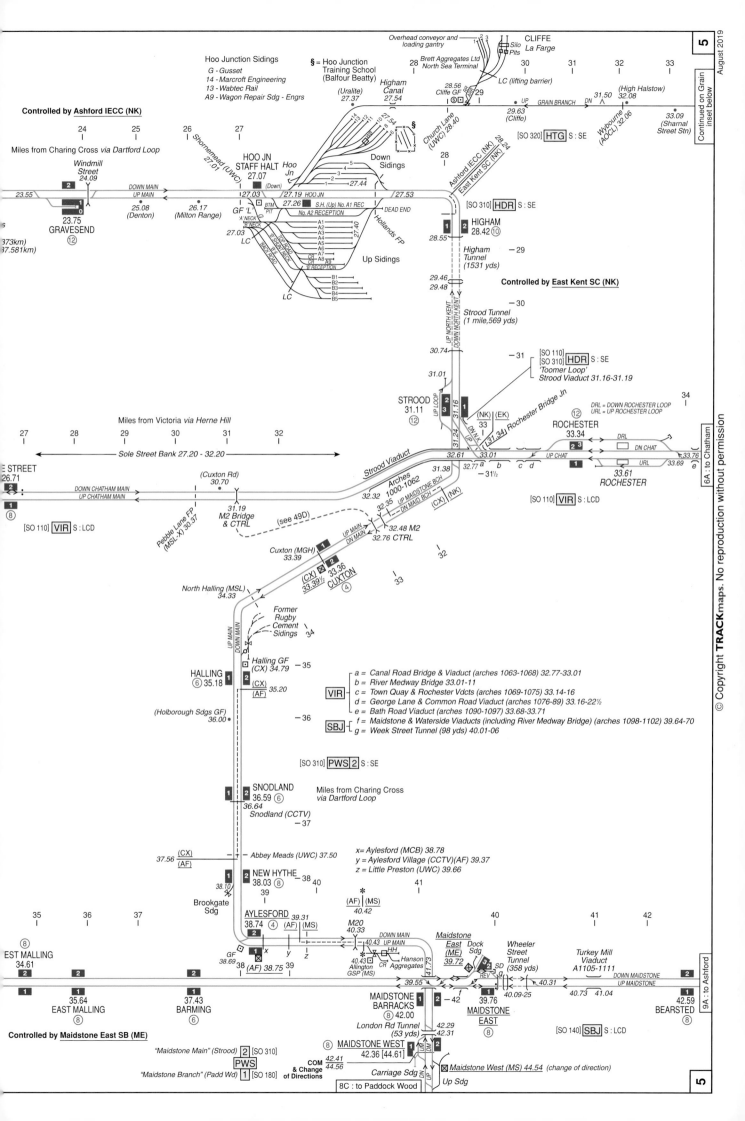

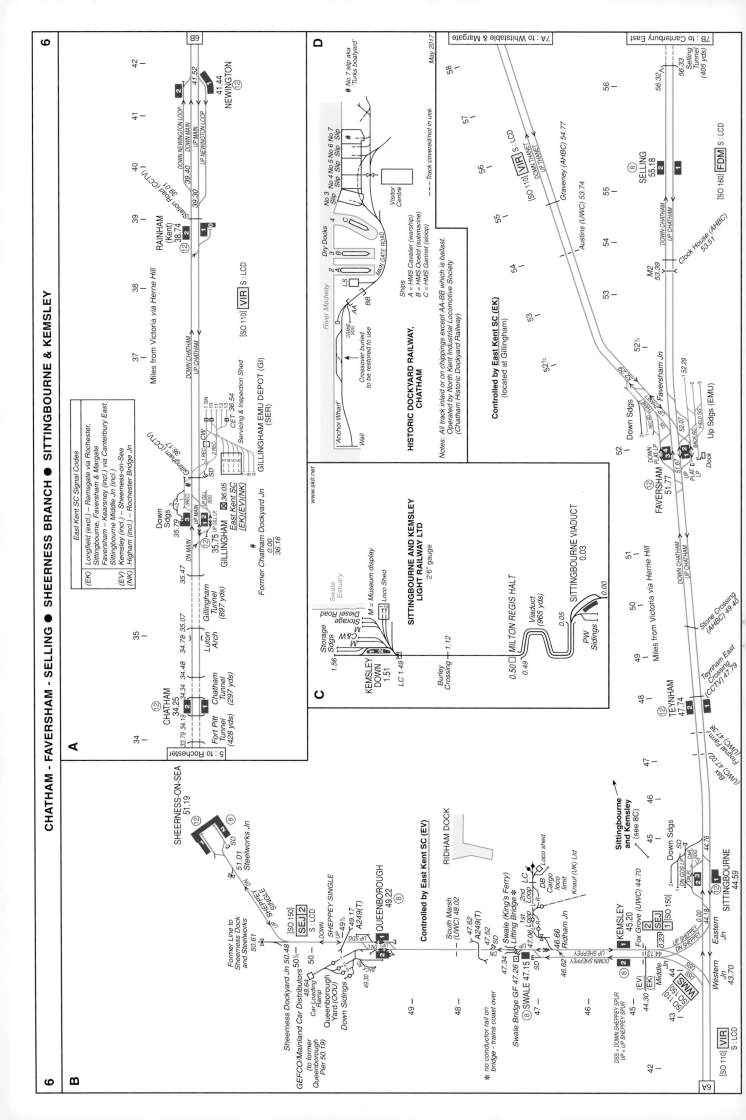

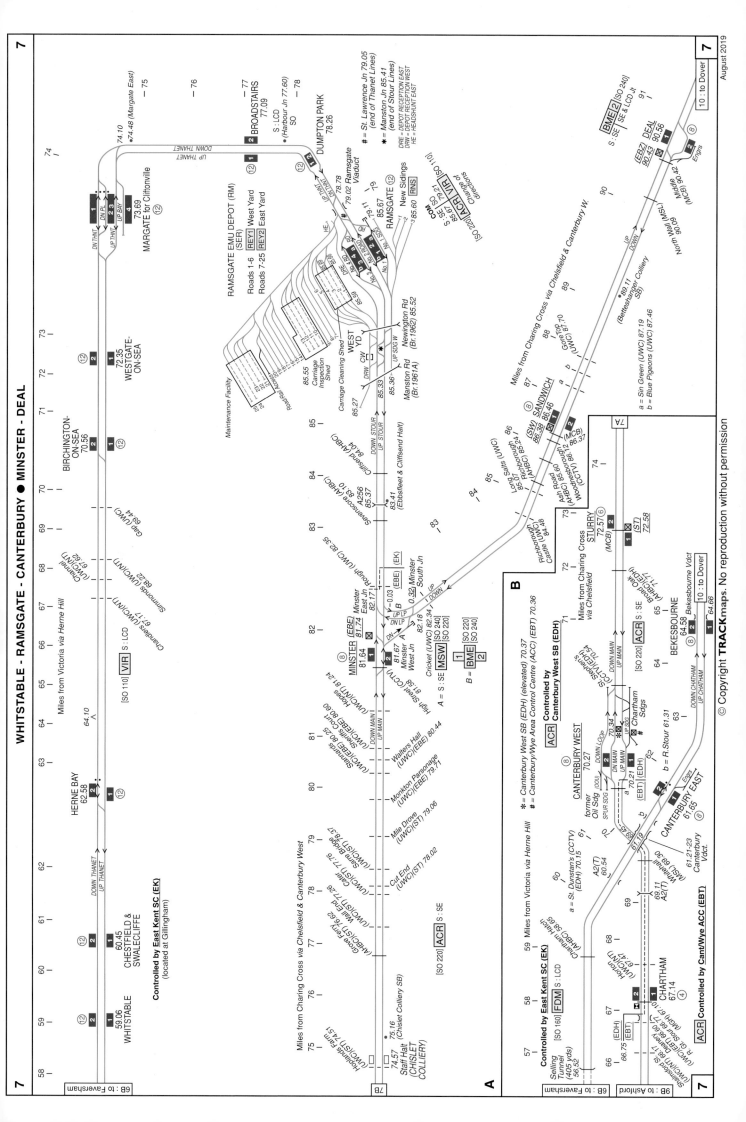

WHITSTABLE - RAMSGATE - CANTERBURY ● MINSTER - DEAL

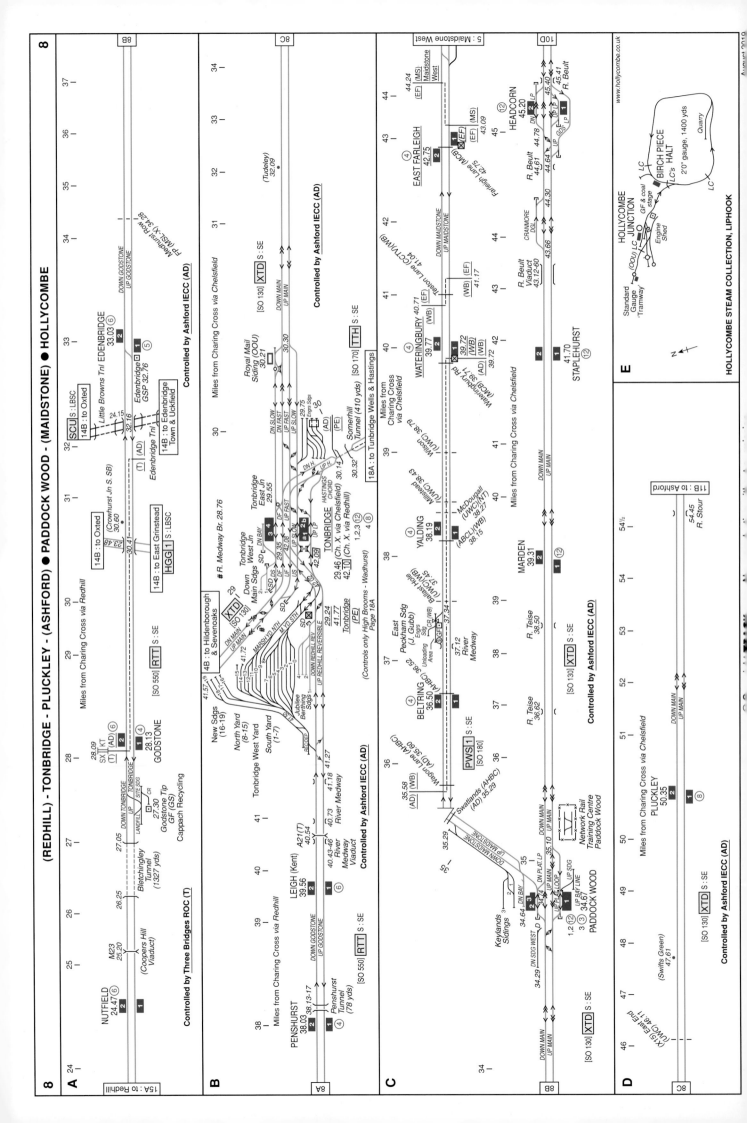

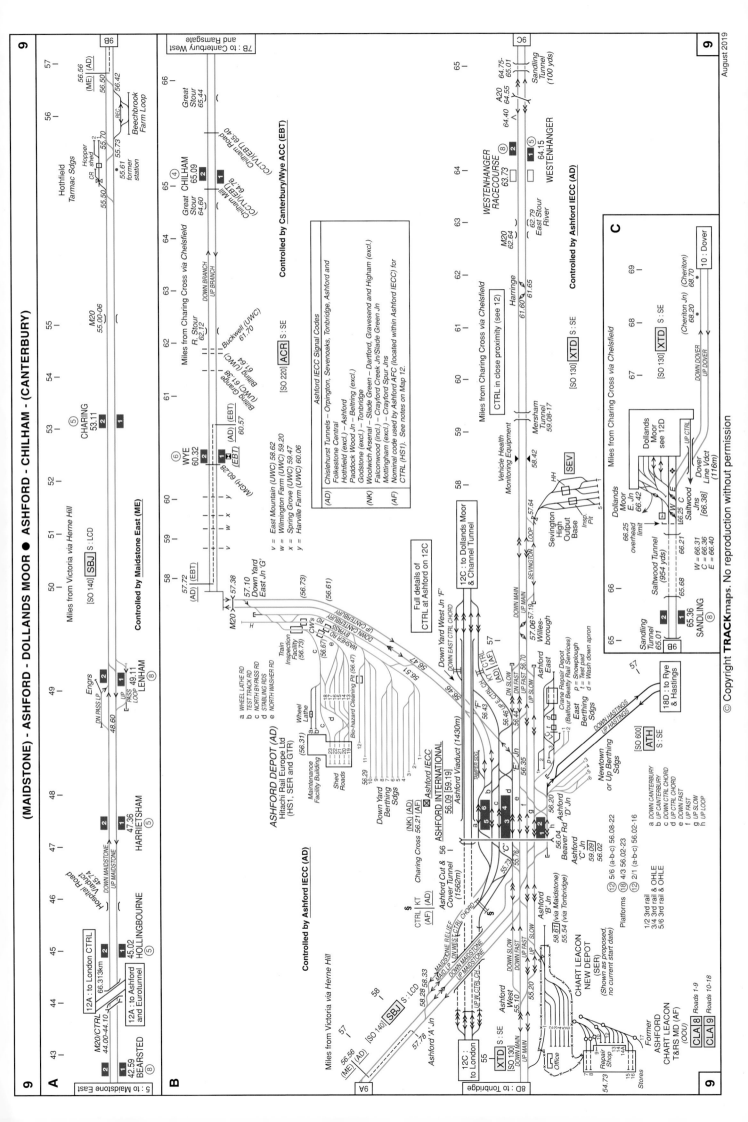

(CANTERBURY) & (DEAL) - DOVER ● FOLKESTONE - DOVER ● EAST KENT RAILWAY

7A : to Deal & Ramsgate

92.27 WALMER ⑧ 1
2

Cold Blow (MSL) 92.54

DOWN DEAL UP DEAL [YE] (EB2) Deal

[SO 240] BME 2
S : SE & LCD Jt

95.05 MARTIN MILL for St. Margaret's Bay 1
2

Miles from Charing Cross via Chelsfield & Canterbury West

[YE] (EB2) Deal

96.25
96.60
Guston Tunnel (1412 yds)
97.44

River Dour 98.46
99.05
DOWN CHAT.
UP CHATHAM [YE]

Charlton Tunnel (265 yds)

Priory Tunnel (158 yds)
Platforms
3 2 1
DOVER PRIORY ⑧ ⑩ ⑫
77.26 (via Canterbury)
77.23 (via Ashford)

Dover Harbour Tunnel (684 yds)

A20(M)
77.65
77.63
77.32
UP CHATHAM
DN CHATHAM
77.16
77.08
76.77
76.65
[SO 160] FDM
S : LCD
[SO 130/160]

Carriage Sdgs

(Hawkesbury Street Jn)

Line description change COM
[SO 130] HSE S : SE
77.76
0.14-76.53
76

UP MAIN
DN MAIN

(Archcliffe Jn)
75.77
76.36
● 76.54 (Old Pilot Tower)
Sea Defence Wall

Shakespeare Tunnels (1387 yds)

SHAKESPEARE Staff Halt
75.14
75.09
DOWN MAIN
UP MAIN

Trip wire alarm (down side)

Abbotscliffe Tunnel (1 mile, 182 yds)
74.32
73.23

75
74
73

Buckland Jn 76.32
DOWN CHAT. UP CHATHAM [YE]

[EK] [YE]
2
1 KEARSNEY ⑧ 75.09

Kearsney Viaduct 74.78

[EK] [YE]

Controlled by East Kent SC (EK)
(located at Gillingham)

EAST KENT RAILWAY
www.eastkentrailway.co.uk

73.58 Wigmore Lane
73.27
Eastry
73.24 EYTHORNE
EKR (TMOG)
LC
Golgotha Tunnel (477 yds)
72.10-31
North Bank (MCG) 0.75/71.75
0.72
SHEPHERDS WELL 0.55
Lydden Tunnel (1 mile, 609 yds)
73.15

Former BR connection
NR/EKR 71.46
71.04
Down Sdgs 71.39
LONG SDG
0.51
SHEPHERDS WELL ⑧ 71.60
1

70 Miles from Victoria I via Herne Hill

Three Arch Viaduct 67.35

DOWN CHATHAM
CHATHAM MAIN

ADISHAM ⑧ 67.60
1
2
[SO 160] FDM S : LCD

AYLESHAM ⑧ 68.66
1
2

SNOWDOWN ⑧ 69.60
1
2

Controlled by Folkestone East SB (YE)

Miles from Charing Cross via Chelsfield

(Warren Staff Halt) 72.02

Martello Tunnel (532 yds)
71.47
71.22
2 71.22 Train Roads (14 cars)
Berthing Sdgs (14 cars)
2
3
3

FOLKESTONE EAST Staff Halts
1=70.73
2=71.01 SB (YE) 70.79
70.72

[SO 230] S : SE
1
FFH
2

71.08 *
71.08 *
(AD) [YE]
§
71.25

[AD] [YE]
P
P
P
#

* = Mileage reversal
§ = Sections of track removed from Up Folkestone Harbour Branch
▼ = Harbour Vdct. (Arches 1154-1135)
= Folkestone Harbour incline (1:30)

Ø = rails intact but not useable - track beyond fence - public walkway

[SO 130] XTD S : SE

FOLKESTONE WEST
69.22 ⑧
2
1
DOWN DOVER
UP DOVER

(AD) [YE]

[SO 130] XTD S : SE
FOLKESTONE CENTRAL ⑫
70.27-39
70.72
2 1
69.73

Folkestone or Foord Vdct.

71.71 71.63
(OOU) UP FOLK HARB
(OOU) DN FOLK HARB

Swing Br.
Radnor Vdct.

closed (EBB)
FOLKESTONE HARBOUR 72.07
72.02

7B : to Canterbury East
9C : to Sandling & Ashford

© Copyright TRACK ...
71 72 73 74 75 76 (mileposts)
65 66 67 68 69 70 71 72

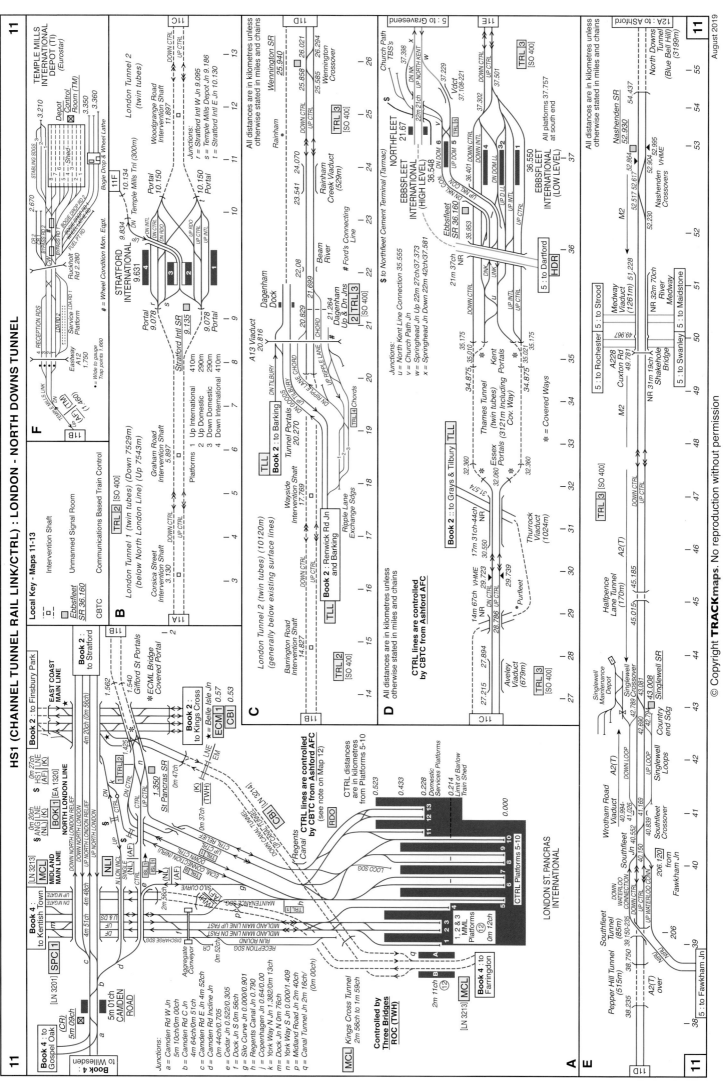

HS1 (CHANNEL TUNNEL RAIL LINK/CTRL) : LONDON - NORTH DOWNS TUNNEL

© Copyright **TRACKmaps**. No reproduction without permission

August 2019

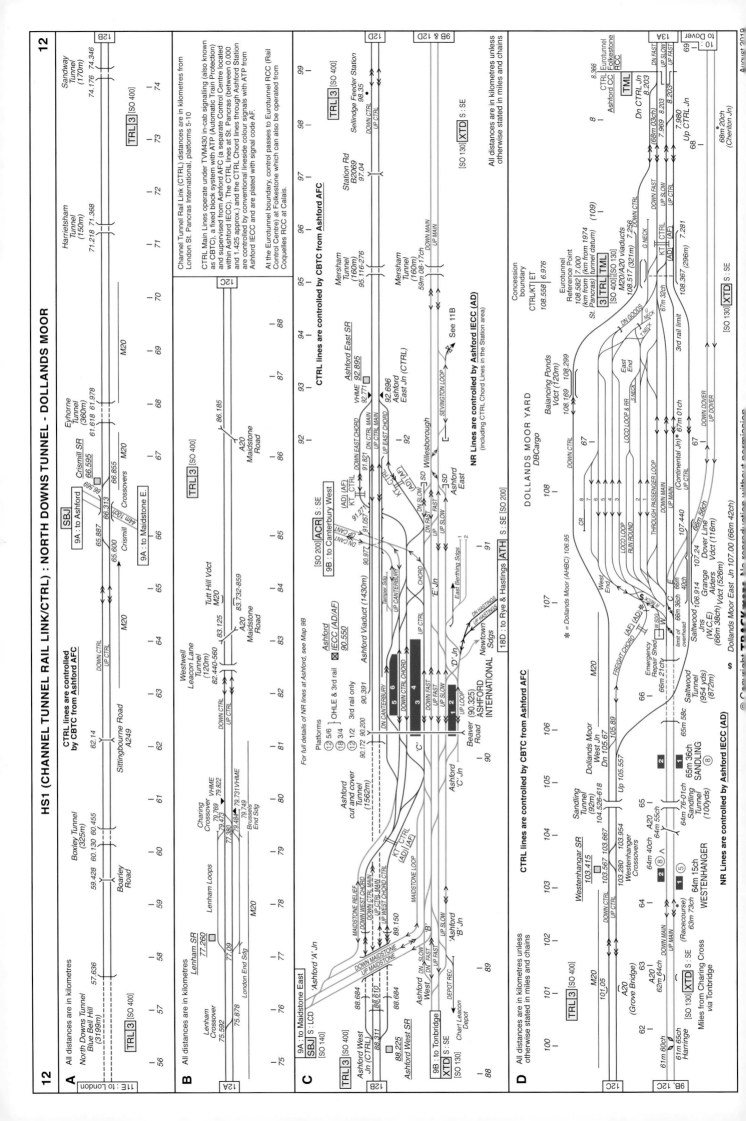

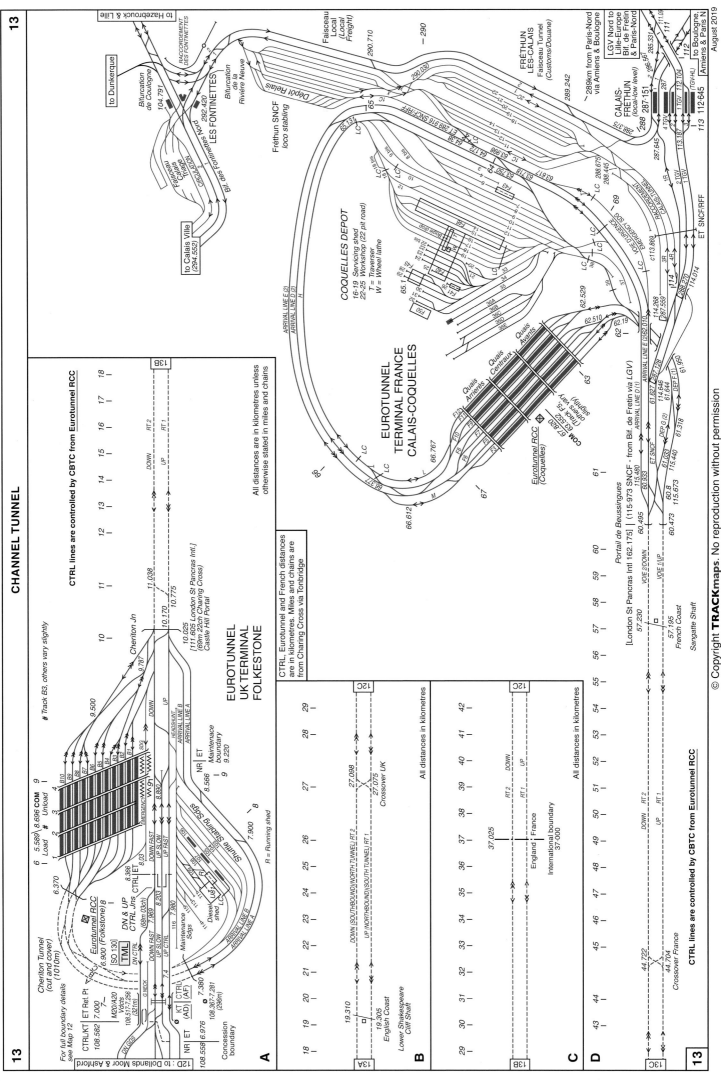

CHANNEL TUNNEL

August 2019

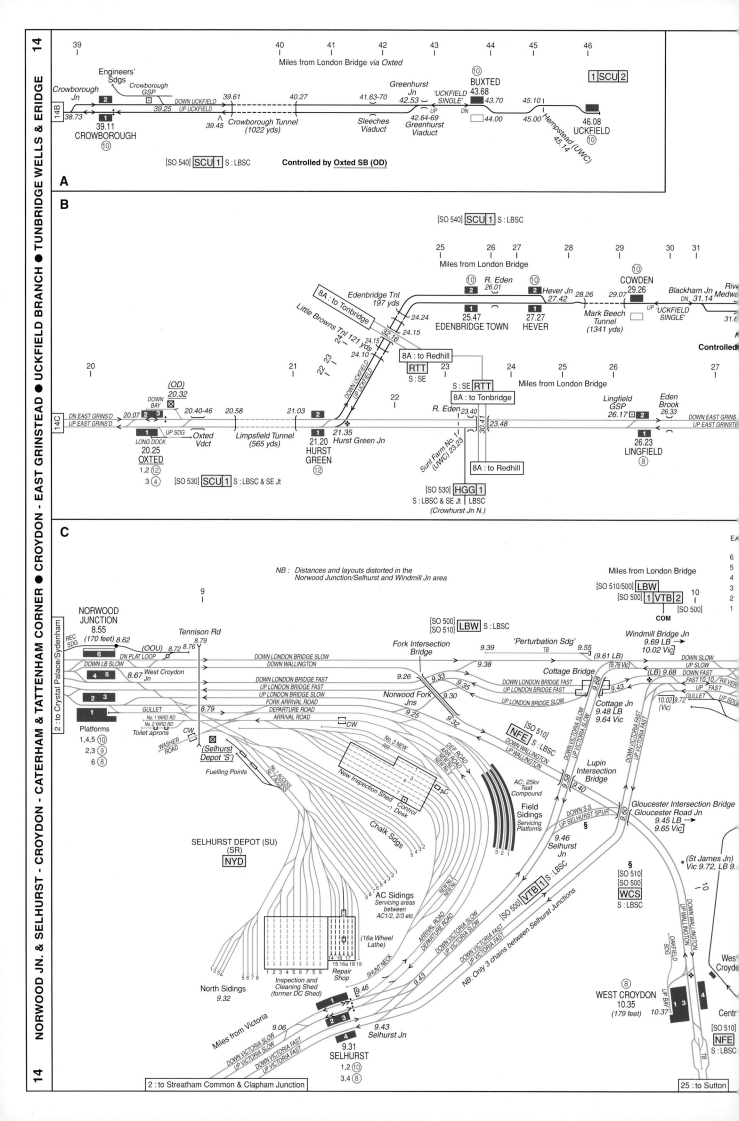

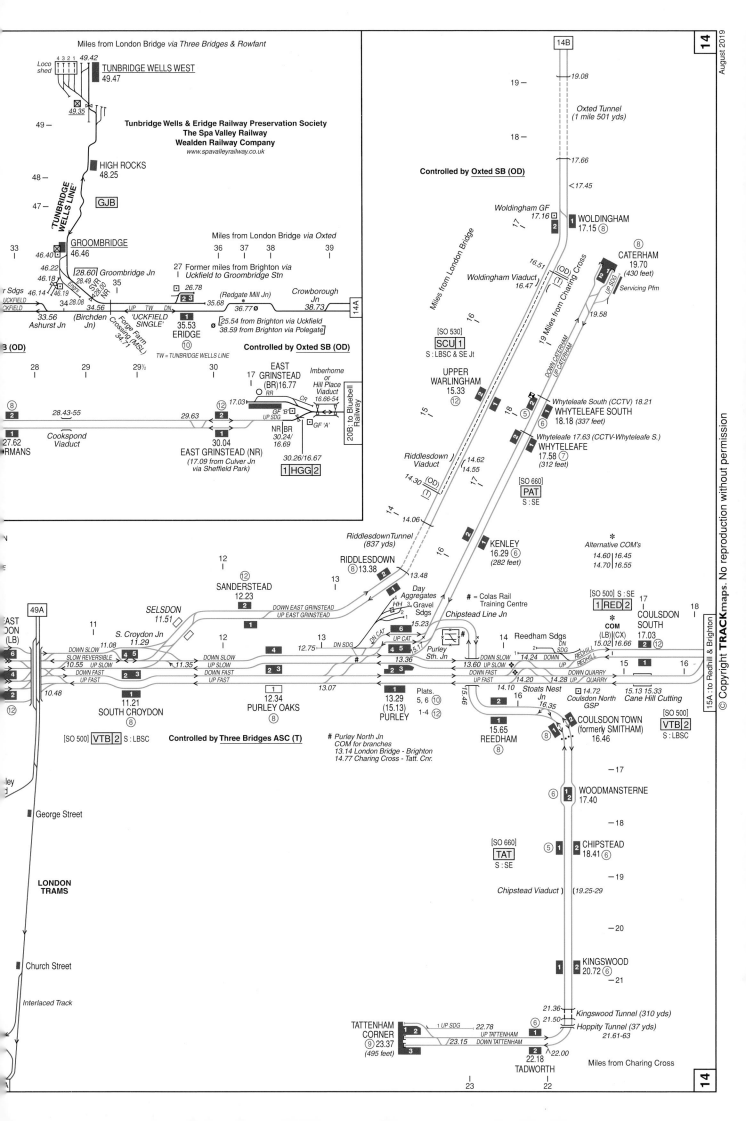

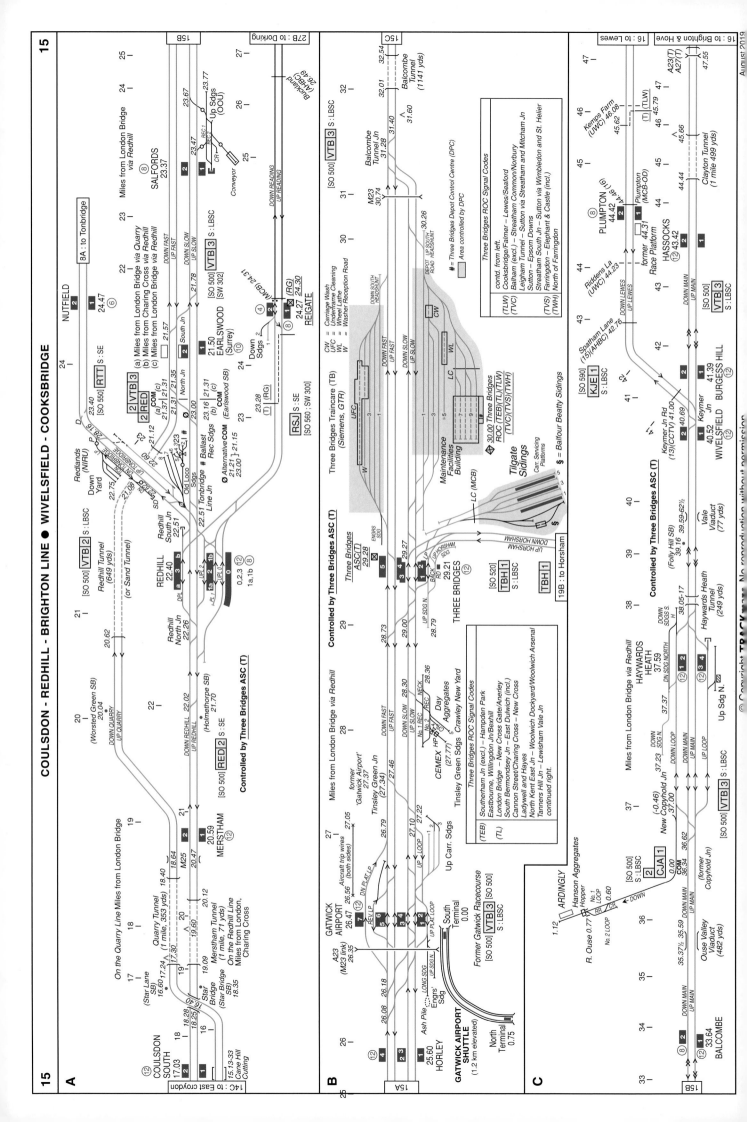

COULSDON - REDHILL - BRIGHTON LINE ● WIVELSFIELD - COOKSBRIDGE

BRIGHTON – HOVE, PRESTON PARK & LEWES ● VOLK'S ELECTRIC RAILWAY

A

THE LAVENDER LINE
c1 mile of track in use
www.lavender-line.co.uk

disused track

River Uck

WORTH HALT 14.38
14.40
– LC 14.28

Lavender Line Preservation Society

Miles from Brighton
–14

SCU 2

B

ISFIELD 13.45
2 13.48

⊠ Proposed signalbox

LC

Shed

Dock

Tramway Loading

Ramp

1

15C : to Haywards Heath

Patcham Tunnel (492 yds)
47.65
48.07
–48

Miles from London Bridge via Redhill
–49

Preston Park Carr. Sdgs

48.74
UP MAIN
DOWN MAIN
UP LOOP

[SO 500] VTB 3 S : LBSC

PRESTON PARK 49.21 ⑫
3

Preston Park Jn 49.43

49.35

49.56

Cliftonville Tunnel (535 yds)
50.00

[SO 500] [SO 630] PPH S : LBSC

UP CLIFTONVILLE SPUR
DOWN CLIFTONVILLE SPUR

50.28

50.38
1.18
1.15

50.48 Hove Jn
1.28

HOVE
(50.56)
1.35
3
1.47
1.08

Hove Carr. Sdgs (SR)
50.69
50.78

UP LOOP
1.57
UP BTN
DOWN BTN
1.58

Sackville Road

Carriage servicing platforms

23A : to Worthing

Miles from Brighton

1
1¾

15C : to Keymer Jn

COOKSBRIDGE 47.31 ⑥
1 47.35
2 (18)(CCTV)

KJE 1 S : LBSC
[SO 590] 48

Lewes Tunnel (395 yds)
49.49
49.67

DOWN LEWES
UP LEWES

Hamsey River

Hamsey (19)(AHBC)
48.12
48.49

1 2 Lewes Jn 50.03/8.03
1
2 3
4 5 PLAT LP 8.08

LEWES 49.74 ⑦
7.77

1, 2 ⑫
3, 4 ⑦
5 ⑦

LUS = LEWES UP SIDING

Kingston Tunnel (107 yds)
7.13-18

(TLW) 7.08
(TLW) 6.50
(Ashcombe SB) 5.76
A27(T)

4.62 (TLW)
4.05

17A : to Newhaven & Eastbourne

Controlled by Three Bridges ROC (TLW)

[SO 620] BTL S : LBSC

Falmer Tunnel (490 yds)
4.20
3.62

FALMER 3.39 ⑧
1
2
3.60

Miles from Brighton

Hodshrove Viaduct

MOULSECOOMB 1.65 ④
1
2

DOWN EAST BRANCH
UP EAST BRANCH

Ditching Road Tunnel (63 yds)
0.66
•(Kemp Town Jn)
•(Kemp Town Jn) 0.63

LONDON ROAD (Brighton) 0.57 ⑦
1
2

London Road Viaduct (390 yds)
0.44
0.26
0.23 (Goods Incline)
0.31 Montpelier Jn 0.13
¥ Montpelier Sdgs

Controlled by Three Bridges ASC (T)

[SO 500] VTB 3 S : LBSC

49.49
1.2 = GTR Servicing platform
49.57

49.73 Dyke Road

CW 49.79
GOODS RECEPTION
⊞ GSP
Engrs Sdg

LOCO REL

[SO 500] VTB 3 S : LBSC

49.75
50.00
UP MAIN
DOWN MAIN
CARRIAGE ROAD NORTH
CARRIAGE ROAD

CARR RD S

49.65 CW
49.74 Lovers Walk (L)
WASHER RD
NORTH SDG No.1
N SDG 2
LW 2
N SDG 1
W. CARR RD
WEST LP

BPJ

BRIGHTON T & RS MD (BI) (SR)

Lovers Walk Inspection & Cleaning Shed

Cleaning platforms

Engrs Depot Sdg

Wall Sdgs
0.10

Hove Tunnel (220 yds)
0.40
0.30
0.05/50.42 Brighton West Coast Jn

[SO 630] BLI 1 S : LBSC
[SW 305]

0.75 (Holland Rd)

1 (LOVERS WALK No.3) Snow & Ice
$ BREAKDOWN CRANE
⊠ (LOVERS WALK No.3) Snow & Ice
Brighton West Coast Jn 0.05/50.42

BLI 1

BRIGHTON
1 2 3 4 5 6 7 8

50.48
50.49 VTB 3
0.00 (-0.04) BTL

0.00 ⑧
Platforms
⑫ ③ 4-8
② ⑧ ④

C VOLK'S ELECTRIC RAILWAY
(Brighton & Hove City Council)
Gauge : 2'8½" (825mm), 110V dc, third rail
www.volkselectricrailway.co.uk

AQUARIUM 0.00
viaduct

LC No.13 (A)
LC No.12 (A)
LC No.11 (A)
LC No.10 (A)
West Loop
LC No.9 (A)
LC No.8 (C)
Beach Sports Centre
LC No.7 (C)

PASTON PLACE (Halfway) 0.44
Workshop & power plant
Carr. Shed

LC No.6 (C)
LC No.5 (C)
Banjo Groyne 5
LC No.4 (B)
East Loop
LC No.3 (B)
LC No.2 (D)

MARINA (BLACK ROCK) 1.02

Brighton Beach

Volk's Railway Crossing Types
(A) = Pedestrian, fixed red lights, gated.
(B) = Pedestrian, fixed red lights, open.
(C) = User worked, gated – no.7 fixed red lights, nos 5 & 6 red/yellow flashing lights, no.8 red flashing lights.
(D) = Pedestrian, fixed red lights, open landward side, gated seaward side.

August 2019

© Copyright TRACKmaps. No reproduction without permission

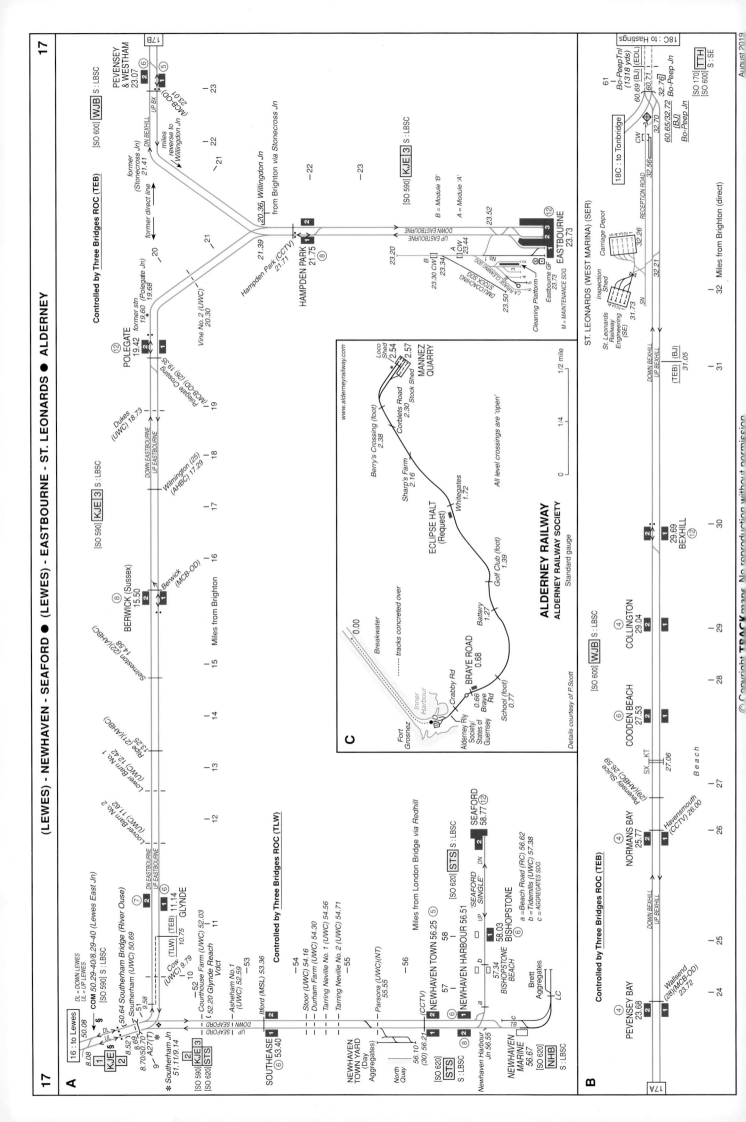

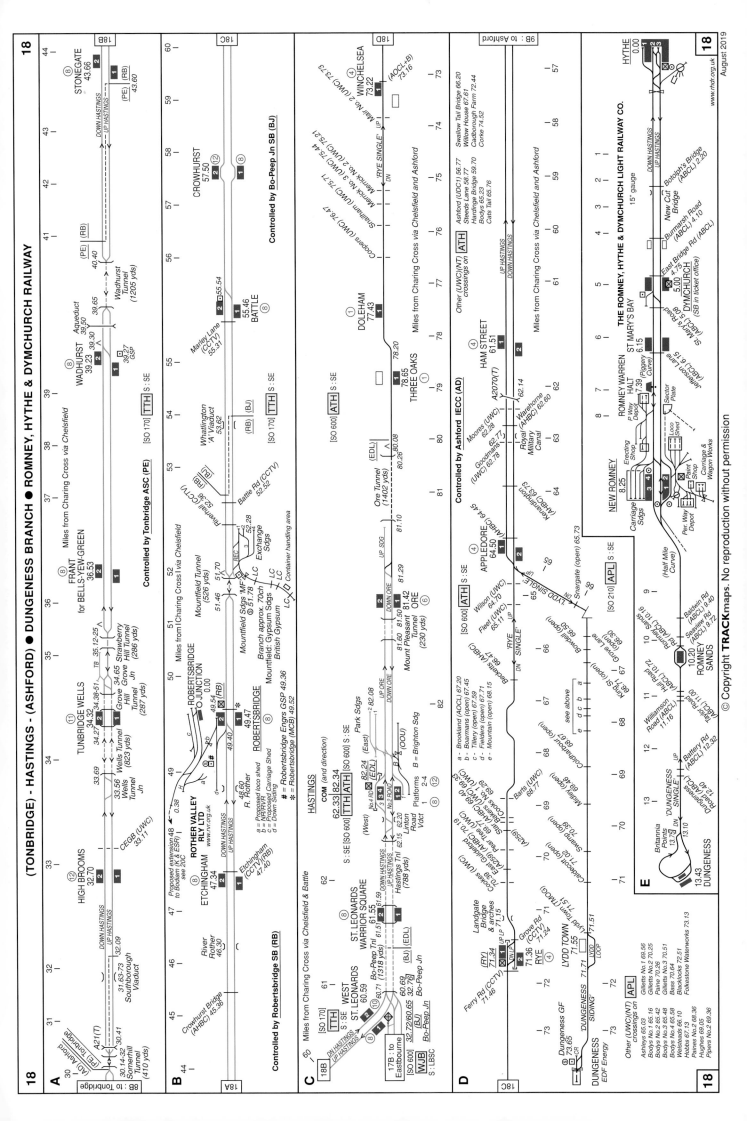

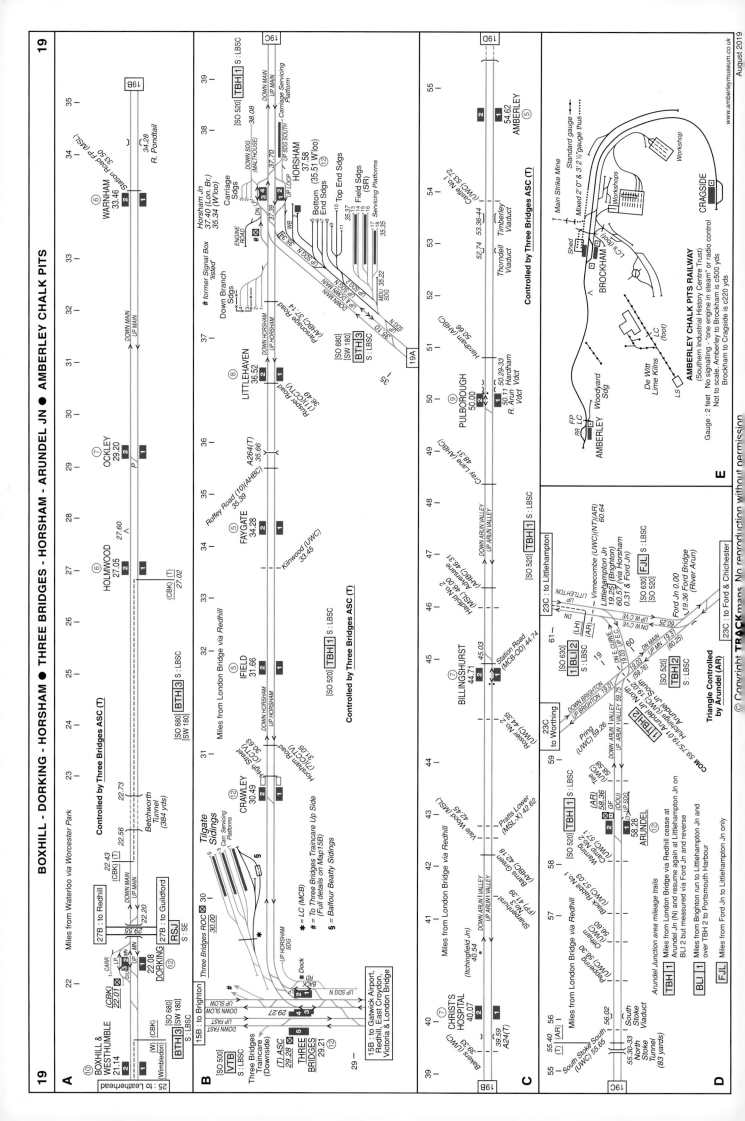

ISLE OF WIGHT ● BLUEBELL RAILWAY ● KENT & EAST SUSSEX RLY ● SWANAGE RAILWAY

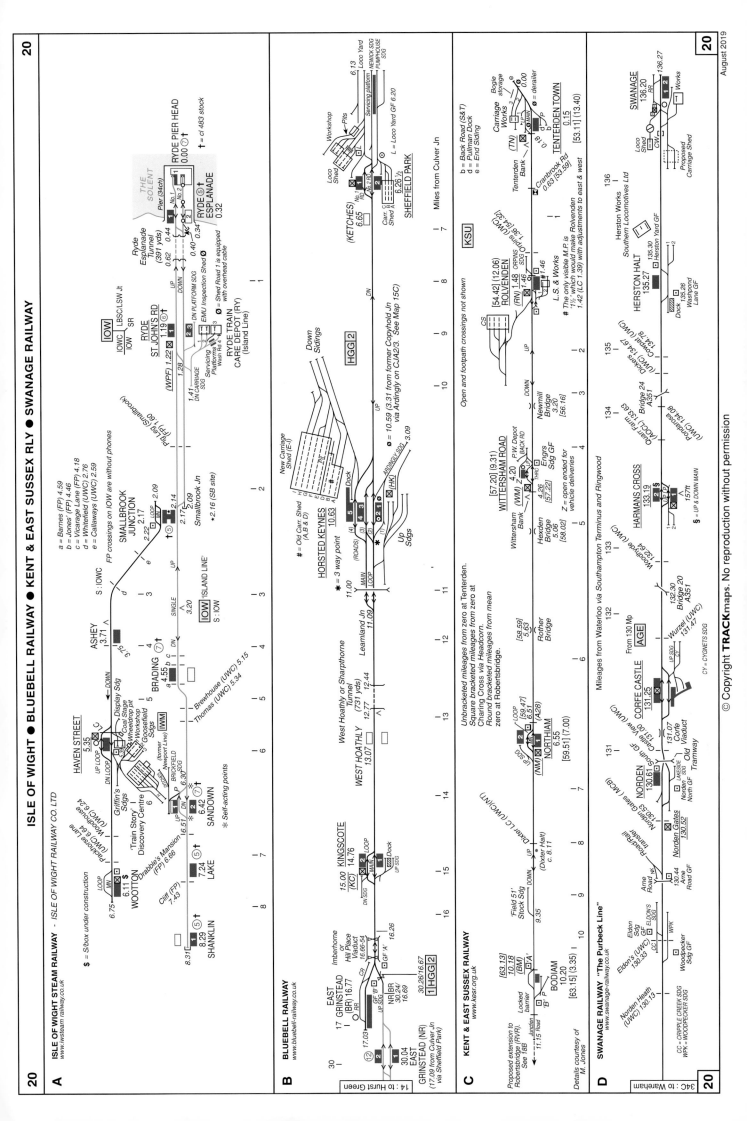

A **ISLE OF WIGHT STEAM RAILWAY** - ISLE OF WIGHT RAILWAY CO. LTD
www.iwsteam-railway.co.uk

B **BLUEBELL RAILWAY**
www.bluebell-railway.co.uk

C **KENT & EAST SUSSEX RAILWAY**
www.kesr.org.uk

D **SWANAGE RAILWAY** "The Purbeck Line"
www.swanage-railway.co.uk

August 2019

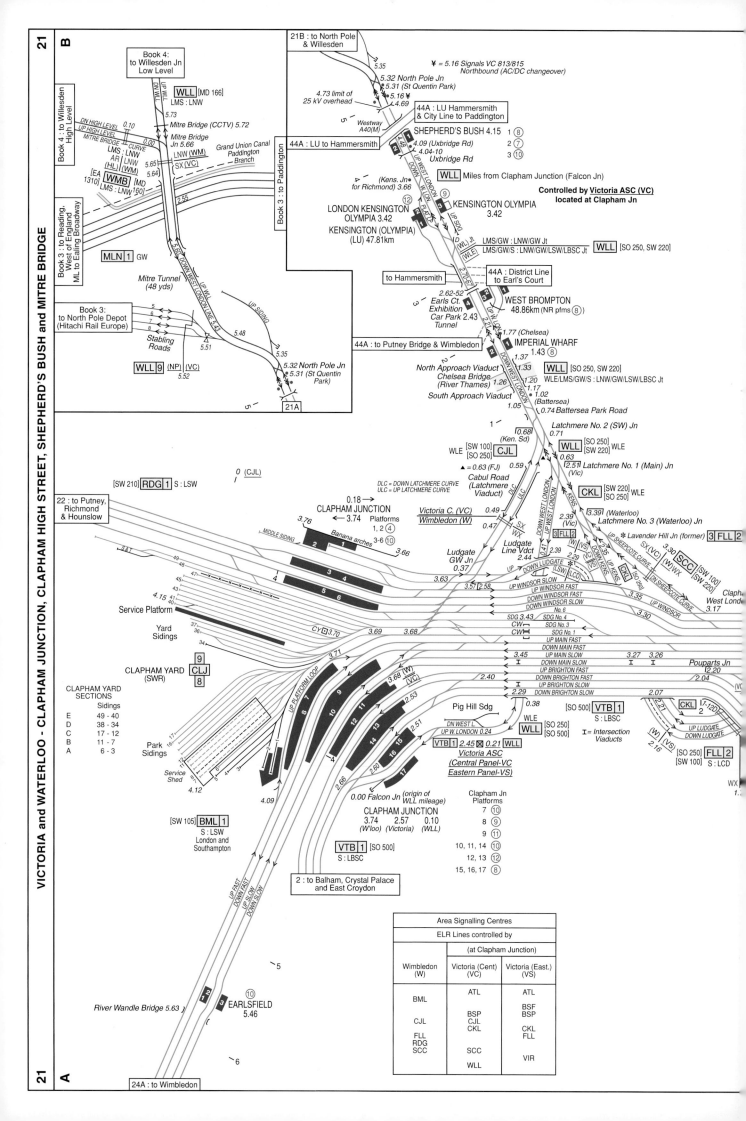

LONDON VICTORIA
0.00

LONDON WATERLOO 0.05 (Mileage origin 0.00 at junction with former SE Rly)

7 6 5 4   0.00 (4-7)
0.01 (2 & 3)
3 2   0.03 (8)
13 12 11 10 9
8
15 14
0.05
Platforms
0.04 (9-13)
1 ⑬   0.06 (14-15)
2 ⑭   0.08 (16-19)
19 18 17 16
3,4 ⑧
5-6 ⑫/10N
7 ⑬
8 ⑩
9-19 ⑫
= Networker Stock

24 23 22 21 20   19 18   17 16 15 14   13 12 11 10   9 8   7 6 5 4 3 2 1   0.06
0.07
NB: Slight chainage variations occur with buffer stop locations
Platforms
1 - 6 ⑩
7 - 16 ⑫
17 ⑬
18 - 24 ⑫
0.14

Eccleston Bridge 0.10

Elizabeth Bridge 0.21

[SO 500] VTB 1   VIR (VS)   RDG 1
S : LBSC   S : LCD   [SW 100]

Outbound Gantry 0.28

Ebury Bridge 0.33

Up Carriage Sdgs (Pugs Hole)
Inbound Gantry 0.35

Last Up Signal Gantry
Waterloo Viaduct (222-285) (-279 RDG)
0.00-0.24
0.24
Music Hall Vdct. (214A-221)
0.27
Necropolis Vdct. (208A-214)

* = Trap point wide to gauge

Controlled by Victoria ASC (VC)
located at Clapham Junction

Victoria (Grosvenor) Carriage Shed
0.51
'A'   'B' Section

Controlled by Victoria ASC (VS)
located at Clapham Junction

Controlled by Wimbledon ASC (W)

First Down Signal Gantry 0.34

0.32
Classics Viaduct (204A-208)
0.33
0.35
Carlisle Viaduct (191-204)

0.58

Grosvenor Bridge (River Thames) 0.65

West Crossings 0.39
International Jn 0.40

Carlisle Lane Jn 0.42

0.41   —1/2

0.70 (arch 759)
Battersea Pier Sidings Staff Halt 0.72
0.71 (arch 759)
0.72
a   Battersea Pier Jn 0.78 (arch 742)
0.73
0.48
Union Flag Vdct. (176-190)
0.55
Spread Eagle Vdct. (165-175)
Signal Box Vdct. (156-164)
0.60

Battersea Pier Sdgs
1.01
0.78
[SO 110] BSF   S : LCD
(724)
b
0.68
Newport St. Vdct. (140-155)
Whitgift Viaduct (130-139)
0.73
Granby Viaduct (122-129)

1.05
1.05
(arch 723)

a = Spicers Wharf Viaduct
b = Engine Viaduct
c = Battersea Dogs' Home Viaduct
d = Havelock Terrace Viaduct
e = Pagden Street Viaduct
f = Gladstone Terrace Viaduct

0.77
Randall Road V. (106A-121)
—1

Battersea Park Jn
Platforms
2 ⑤
3 ⑩
4,5 ⑧

BATTERSEA PARK 1.23
Viaduct (arches 50B-100)

[SW 100] VTB 1   [SO 500] VTB 1
RDG 1   S : LBSC
S : LSW

c
(arch 714) (arch 713)
1.18
1.23
d
1
7.27 (Lon. Br.)
1 BSP
ATL LBSC
VIR (VS) [SO 110]

1.26
[SO 645]   BSF [SO 110]
[SO 250]
VAUXHALL 1.29
1.04
Tinworth St V. (100-106)
1.08
Glasshouse Walk V. (88-99)
1.13
Guinness Viaduct (76-87)
1.19
White Lion Viaduct (67-75)

QUEENSTOWN RD (Battersea)
e

* BML 1 Wheel Chex 2.44 UMF and UMS

[SW 100] RDG 1 S : LSW

1.23
Goding Street Viaduct (58-66)
1.27
Vauxhall Station Viaduct (45-57)

50B
50B
1/2 2.50
1
(NIRU)
y

f (696)
1.30
1.35
WINDSOR REV.
UP WINDSOR CURVE
DN WATERLOO CURVE
Nine Elms Jn 1.78 WIN REV
2.0

1.35
Rowton House Viaduct (39-44B)
1.39
Coronation Viaduct (19-38C)

WINDSOR REVERSIBLE
UP WINDSOR
DOWN WINDSOR FAST
DOWN WINDSOR SLOW
UP MAIN FAST
DOWN MAIN FAST
UP 3M. SLOW
1.67
UP BATT. SX 1.67 KT
BATTERSEA
UP KEN. 1.67
SINGTON

2.65
2.61
UP WINDSOR
7.12
2.50 U.M.F
(BML)
2.61 Q'town Rd V.
Longhedge Jns (C,B,A)
2.52

arches 692-695
S : LBSC

2.42 2.38
1.31 (VIR)
DN WIN.S
2.50 U.M.F
UP M.S
DN M.S

WINDSOR REV.
DN W.F
DN W.S
UP M.F
DN M.F
UP M.S
DN M.S

1.48
Brand's Viaduct (arches 1-18B)

2.37 Up
2.31 (W)
(VS) Down

2.49-13
Nine Elms International flyover

2.08 Nine Elms Viaduct (arches 1-72)
1.59

[SW 100] BML 1 S : LSW

1.63 (B)
(C)
Longhedge Jn
1.47
1.58
49A 0.09
DOWN BRIGHTON FAST
DOWN BRIGHTON SLOW
DOWN BRIGHTON SLOW
1.56
1.62 (A)
T.62 (A)
BATTERSEA
1.52
x
ø
AHG BR
Stewarts Lane Viaduct
[SW 100] [SO 110]

1.36
1.38
NIRU
NIRU
1.38
1.41
CW
12.44
ø
Stewarts Lane Jn
1
2

FLL Viaducts from Longhedge Jn (A) to Factory Jn
Arches
h = Coal Sidings Viaduct (339)   0.16 - 0.19   84 - 82
k = Old Loco Sdgs Viaduct (340)   0.19 - 0.20   81 - 77
l = South London Line Viaduct (341)   0.22 - 0.25   76 - 70
m = Old Goods Sdgs Viaduct (342)   0.26 - 0.41   69 - 56

2 FLL 1
Viaduct (arches 79X-84X)
h
BSP 2 [SO 250] [SO 500]

1.45 (Vic.), 2.50 (Wat.) Linford Street Jn

Linford St./Pensbury Place Viaduct 1.38-1.68

STEWARTS LANE
Traction & Rolling Stock Maintenance Depot (SL)
SLC

[SO 250] FLL 1 S : LCD

ATL Viaducts from Shepherds Lane Jn to Battersea Park Stn
Arches
s = Voltaire Road Viaduct   6.15 - 6.17   641 - 644A
t = Portslade Road Viaduct   6.56 - 6.17   1 - 22
u = Carriage Shed Viaduct   6.75 - 7.00   23 - 43
w = Stewarts Lane Viaduct   7.00 - 7.06   44 - 49
x = Ingate Place Viaduct   7.06 - 7.12   50 - 58
y = Patcham Terrace Viaduct   7.13 - 7.18   59 - 73
z = Battersea Park Viaduct   7.22 - 7.26   74 - 80

6.63
SX
KT
u

VIR [SO 110] S : LCD
1.55 arch 645

Factory Junctions
ELR   ATL   BSF   FLL   VIR
A   6.58   1.75   -   1.68
B   6.67   1.67   -   (1.75)
C   6.67   1.67   0.41   1.67

VIR Viaducts from Clapham High St. Stn to Shepherds Lane Jn
Arches
p = Voltaire Road Viaduct   2.29 - 2.32   644A - 641
q = Lendal Terrace Viaduct   2.32 - 2.37   640 - 631
r = Cottage Grove Viaduct   2.37 - 2.39   630 - 628A

Longhedge Junctions
ELR   BSP   FLL   CKL
A   1.58   0.09   1.63
B   1.63   1.67
C   1.67   1.67

SLC 8
Carriage Servicing and Inspection Shed

SLC 9

Wandsworth Road Jn 6.58

arch 649
1.68
Factory Junctions

Miles from Victoria (E) via Chatham Main Line

[SO 110] VIR S : LCD

2 : to Brixton, Herne Hill, Elephant & Castle, Peckham Rye, & Nunhead

1.67
1.61
former Goods Yard

WANDSWORTH ROAD
(LB)6.52 (1.75)(Vic)

Voltaire Road Jn

2.04
2.03
2.15
6.39

2.25
p q r
Shepherds Lane Jn 2.70 (Vic.) Vdct
DOWN CHATHAM MAIN
UP CHATHAM MAIN
DOWN ATLANTIC (2.62)
UP ATLANTIC
2.78

2 : to Peckham Rye & London Bridge

c = Carriage & wagon shed & Venice-Simplon Orient Express (VSOE) SLC 1

d = Electric loco. running shed with wheel lathe at end of no. 3 road

6.33

CLAPHAM HIGH STREET
(LB)6.21 (2.25)(Vic)

6.14-09 Lendal Terrace Viaduct
6.08-06 Cottage Grove Viaduct
5.68 (London Bridge)
5.50 Shepherds Lane Viaduct

[SO 645] ATL S : LCD

Miles from London Bridge via Denmark Hill

August 2019

21 : to Clapham Junction

0 (CJL)

*~ EAST PUTNEY REVERSIBLE
NR(WX)/LU boundary 5.55
Putney Cutting Viaducts:
Down Line 5.20-48 arches 75-63
Up Line 5.42-48, arches 62-54
Stores Viaduct 5.50-54, arches 45-53

[SW 210] RDG 1 S : LSW

4
3 2
1
8

[PBE] S : LSW Putney W. Tn. Vdct 5.00 4.72
PUTNEY Putney (R. Wandle) Cutting 5.02
5.72 5.09
5.57 5.48 Point Pleasant 4.60
2 3 EAST
UP PUT * Jn PUTNEY 5.60
7.60 NO PPW S : LSW 5
7.53 8 [SW 225]

44A : to Wimbledon
44A : District Line to
Putney Bridge & Earl's Court

EB DISTRICT WB DISTRICT
44A : District Line to Putney Bridge & Earl's Court

[ATG] S : LSW

Wimbledon ASC (W) Controls

BML PBE
CJL part PPW
FLL part RDG part
HOU part

Book 3 : to Paddington

41A : LU Central Line
to White City

* Acton Wells Jn SB (AW) controls
ACW BOK 4&5
AWL CAW

Book 4 : to Cricklewood, Willesden LL/Euston,
Willesden HL

[EA 1310] 4 BOK 5
UP CRICKLEWOOD Acton Wells
DN CRICKLEWOOD 6.76 Jn (AW) 0.64
e MS NO
Book 3 : to Greenford [GW 110] ANL GW WYCOMBE SINGLE MS SO TT
West Ruislip & Ealing Broadway DN 0.72 0.99
[GW 130] AWL [EA 1310] GW EB UP POPLAR
Acton Wells WB DN POPLAR
Book 3 : to Acton East Jn [EA 1310] WR 0.39 AR
and Yard DOWN POPLAR 0.49

GW MLN 1 [GW 103]

e = LNW/WM/ MD 165 / [EA 1360]
AR (AW)
f = 8.ZZ/ 7.03 (St Pancras)
g = 0.66 Acton Wells Jn
LZ QZ/ Falcon Jn
(0.58 Willesden HL Jn)

5.00
Acton West

45C : District Line to Ealing B'way,
Piccadilly Line to Rayners Lane

EB
WB

Book 3 : to Reading,
West of England
ML to Ealing Broadway

45C : District & Piccadilly
Lines to Acton Town

GW routes
ANL [GW 110]
AWL [GW 130]
MLN [GW 103]

Controlled by Thames Valley SC (TVSC)

Churchfield Rd (CCTV) 1.70 4
ACTON CENTRAL 1.73 4
(AC/DC changeover)

2.07 OH Limit

W SOUTH ACTON 2.48 4
2.52 South Acton Jn
SAR 1 [EA 1310]
Bollo Lane (CCTV) 2.63 (Richmond Line)
2.67

To Acton Town

44A : LU District & Piccadilly Line to Hammersmith
[3.12] 9.76
9.53 (51.70km LU) Acton Lane Jn
COM 9.76 Gunnersbury Jn

SAR [EA 1310] 1
2

Miles from Waterloo
via Kensington and
Turnham Green

6 GUNNERSBURY 1
E 2 W 10.05 (52.33km)
W 10.52 9
10.32 W ~11
E 2 W 6
10.43

[SW 230] HOU S : LSW

COM
M 4 3.31 3
A 4 3.35

Kew Bollo Lane
East (Kew Line)
Jn (CCTV)
2.63
DN KEW 3.61
[SW 230] 6 BOK 15 [EA 1310]
LMS : Jn
N & SW COM
Old Kew Jn WX 3.68
(3.68) 10.01
UP KEW WB ~9.34
DOWN HOUNSLOW

Grove Park
(CCTV-F)
8.75

[EA 1310] SAR 2
9.03
UP RICHMOND

[EA 1310]
Bollo Lane (Kew Line) (CCTV)
DN KEW
KEW
BRIDGE
9.53 New Kew Jn
1
10

Miles from Waterloo
via Barnes

BRENTFORD
10.52

10.68
Grand
Jn Canal

Wood Lane (CCTV-F)
11.69

Miles from Waterloo
via Putney

SYON LANE
11.34

ISLEWORTH
12.10

TWICKENHAM
11.22
1 Bay 3
2 BAY
4 5

Twickenham Jn 11.49
11.69

Pope's Grove 11.28
Viaduct and arches, not continuous
ST. MARGARETS
10.66
11.38 11.28

Controlled by Feltham ASC (F)

[SW 210] RDG 1 S : LSW

UP PASS LOOP SD
UP MAIN 12.12 DOWN MAIN
UP MAIN DOWN MAIN

STRAWBERRY HILL 12.22 10
UP STRAW HILL
DN STRAW HILL
24B : to Shepperton

11.49 11

Feltham Jn 13.35
14.38 UP DN
[SW 245] TSJ S : LSW
RDG 1 S : LSW
28A : to Feltham & Staines

HOUNSLOW SPUR
HJW S : LSW
[SW 210]
[SW 230]

HOUNSLOW
13.40

Hounslow
Jn 14.09
River Colne 12.04
1 2
[SW 210] 2
14.39 13.03
14.38 UP

WHITTON
12.43
Whitton Jn
12 13

Miles from Waterloo
via Putney

CHISWICK
8.47

Feltham (W) Wimbledon
8.65 8.39 2
1

BARNES
BRIDGE 7.59
1 2
(R. Thames)
Barnes Br.

White Hart (CCTV) 7.52
Sheen Lane (CCTV) 8.16

MORTLAKE
8.21
10

[SW 210] RDG 1 S : LSW
DOWN RICHMOND
NORTH SHEEN
9.03
8

Richmond
Bridge
(R. Thames)

Oriel Ho. (CCTV-V) 9:12
Umbrella) 9:49
9.63
RICHMOND 1 9.57
7
6 5
4 UP BAY 3 2
Platforms
(SW) 1,2 8
(NL) 3,4,5 6
(LU) 6,7
12.39 (56.16km)

Old Deer Park
Viaduct
10.24 10.08
10.29

KEW GARDENS
11.10 (54.05km)

Richmond
(GB) 12.22
(F) (W)
(GB) [W]
1 [EA 1330] ANG S : LSW
2 [SW 240] WX

1 [EA 1330] 6 BOK 15
2 [SW 230] HOU
Kew Bridge
(River Thames)
9.43 9.64
9.68
9.43 New Kew Jn

BARNES
7.07 2 3
1 7.54
7.67 2

Barnes (Hounslow Rd)
(CCTV/Vine Rd) 7.25
Barnes (Richmond Line)
(Vine Rd)(CCTV) 7.26

Barnes Jn 7.64
7.15
Miles from Mansion House (7.64)
7 8 50.58km
9 1
6.5 6.77 7.71

UP WINDSOR S.
DOWN WINDSOR FAST
DOWN WIN SLOW
UP WINDSOR FAST 2 3

TRACKmaps

© Copyright TRACKmaps. No reproduction without permission

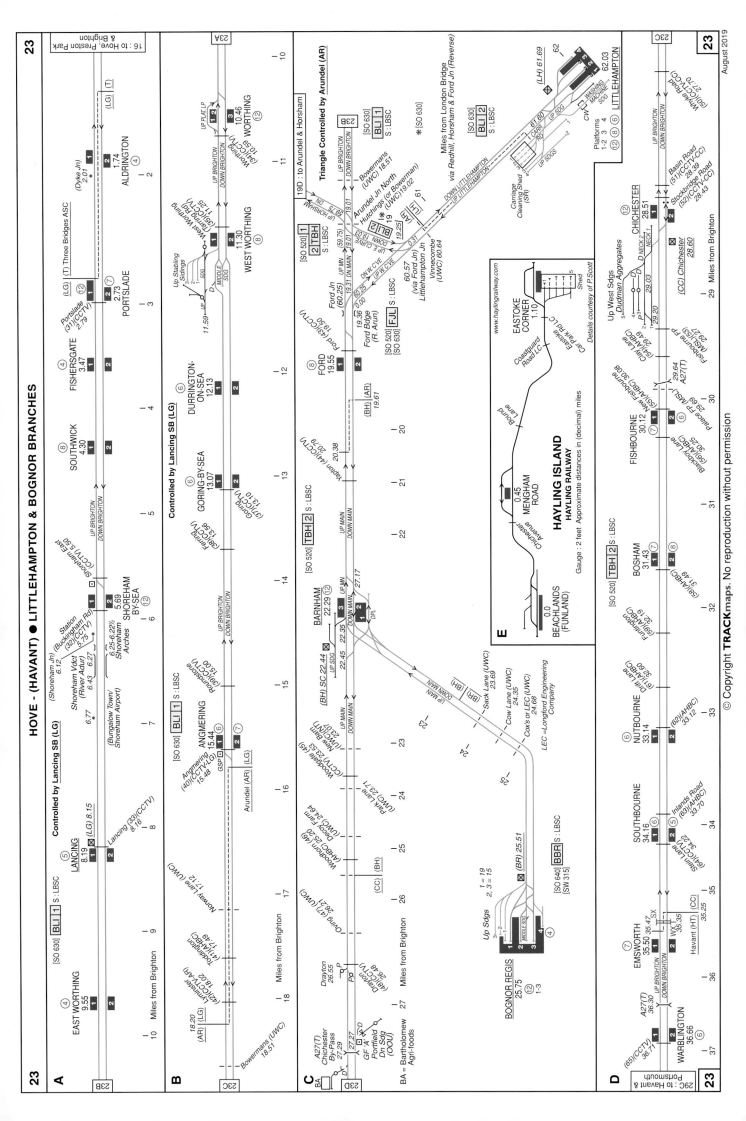

HOVE - (HAVANT) ● LITTLEHAMPTON & BOGNOR BRANCHES

August 2019

A

WIMBLEDON TRAINCARE DEPOT (WD) (SWR)

21: to Clapham Junction

44A: to East Putney & Earl's Ct

WPK

Durnsford Road Sdgs
6.04

Wheel Lathe Shop
6.18

Bogie Drop

Inspection shed

12 & 13 - Lifting Shop
§ = CET Platform
Earlsfield NK Exit

R. Wandle 2 1

EARLSFIELD ⑩ 5.46
3

Sections

25
22
20
18

23

carriage cleaning shed

RUN ROUND No.2 SDG
ACCESS SDG No.2
Durnsford Rd Exit

STAFF HALT

Wimbledon Park Sdgs

WIMBLEDON PARK
7.50 53.59km

[SW 225] PPW S : LSW

Miles from Waterloo via Earlsfield
(Mileage variations exist between Waterloo and Southampton)

DISTRICT LINE
EASTBOUND
WESTBOUND

TY = Wimbledon Top Yard
Shunt Panel (OOU)

Controlled by Three Bridges ROC (TVC) (SMS Lines)

Durnsford Road

R. Wandle
2.07

HAYDONS ROAD ⑧ 2.18
1   2

2: to Tooting, Streatham & Tulse Hill

UP ST.HELIER
DN ST.HELIER

LBSC/LSW Jt

SMS 1

UP SDG 2
UP SDG 1
DOWN SIDING A
DOWN SIDING B

WIMBLEDON
7.19 BML (70 ft)

Wimbledon North Jn
8.26

Wimbledon East 'A' Jns

Platforms 1-4 PPW Buffer stops [55.15km (Ongar)]
(LU services)
Platforms 5-8 BML Centre 7.19 (W'loo via Earlsfield)
Platform 9/10E SMS Centre & BS 3.05 (Streatham S. Jn)
Platforms 9/10E SMS Centre & BS 7.20 (Waterloo via Earlsfield)

Platforms
1 - 4   ⑦
5 - 8   ⑧
9   ⑧
10   ④

'Bridge Ho.
Umbrella'

Wimbledon West (C) Jns

MJW LSW & LBSC Jt

49 : Tramlink to Croydon

Wimbledon Chase 8.13 ⑧

25 : to Sutton

SMS 2

Wimbledon (W) ASC 7.49

RAYNES PARK ⑩ 8.51
1   2

[SW 180] RPE S : LSW
Raynes Park GSP

UP EPSOM
DN EPSOM

25: to Chessington and Epsom

A3 (Kingston Bypass)
9.15

NEW MALDEN 9.62
1   2 3   4

[SW 105] BML 1 S : LSW (London & Soton)

UP SLOW
UP FAST
DOWN FAST
DOWN SLOW

24B

B

Controlled by Feltham ASC (F)

HAMPTON WICK ⑩ 12.44
1   2

Kingston Bridge (River Thames)
12.34

KINGSTON 12.09⑩
1   2   3

Maldens (LU line)

NORBITON ⑩ 11.24
1   2

TEDDINGTON 13.54 ⑩
1   2

COM 12.53

Shacklegate Jn
14.29

[SW 245] TSJ S : LSW

DOWN STRAWBERRY HILL
UP STRAWBERRY HILL No.1 SIDING

CCTV 12.26
Strawberry Hill Jn 12.28

Strawberry Hill 12.22
1   2

Staff crossing 12.33 (foot)

22: to Twickenham

STRAWBERRY HILL DEPOT (ST) (SWR) i/c Siemens

'A' = Carriage Shed
'B' = Commissioning Shed Siemens

[SW 245] SHF S : LSW

HAMPTON COURT 14.76 ⑩
1   2

Hampton Court Jn
14.35

Staff crossing (MSL)

THAMES DITTON 14.01 ⑩

Hampton Court Jn 14.32

[SW 105] BML 1 S : LSW

HAM [SW 195]

2 NMS 1 [SW 190] S : LSW

FULWELL ⑩ 12.75
1

Fulwell Jn

Fulwell Tunnels (Wellington Rd) 13.03-06

HAMPTON ⑩ 14.47
1   2

Percy Rd (CCTV) 14.52

Controlled by Feltham ASC (BEF)

UPPER HALLIFORD 17.34
1

KEMPTON PARK 16.28
1   2

SUNBURY PARK 16.64
1   2

[SW 255] VWW S : LSW

[SW 190] NMS 2 S : LSW

SHEPPERTON 18.73
1   2 3   4

Ash River Bridge
18.46

18.65 DOWN SDG

Miles from Waterloo via Twickenham

UP SLOW
UP FAST
DOWN FAST
DOWN SLOW

Controlled by Woking ASC (WK)

BERRYLANDS ⑩
1   2

Woking (WK) 11.19

Berrylands Jn 11.19

SURBITON 12.03 ⑩
1   2   3 4

HAMPTON COURT Jn
12.40   12.23

[SW 105] BML 1 S : LSW (L & Soton)

HAM [SW 195]

DN COBHAM

vdct-arches FA42-FA1

[SW 200] NGL [SW 195] HAM S : LSW

HINCHLEY WOOD 14.04 ⑩

25: to Effingham Junction

ESHER ⑩ 14.31
1   2 3   4

HERSHAM 15.73 ⑩
1   2

River Mole 15.23

WALTON-ON-THAMES 17.06 ⑫
1   2

Longford River 18.66

WEYBRIDGE 19.12 ⑫
1   2   3

River Wey Viaduct 19.54-52

GSP 19.33

25A: to Virginia Water

River Wey Vdct 19.74 Addlestone Jn

BYFLEET & NEW HAW 20.32 ⑫
1   2

Wey Navigation Canal 20.56

Hogsmill River 10.78

M25 20.53

[SW 255] AJB Byfleet 20.67

WEST BYFLEET 21.54 ⑫
1   2 3

26: to Woking

Miles from Waterloo

August 2019

© Copyright **TRACK**maps. No reproduction without permission

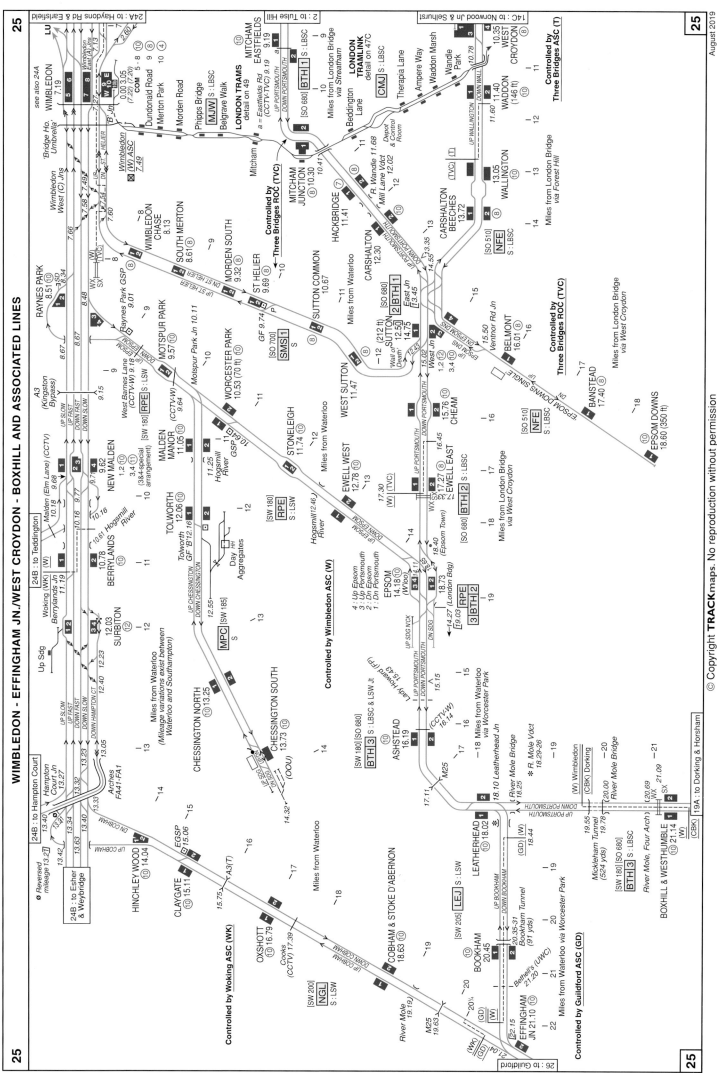

WIMBLEDON - EFFINGHAM JN./WEST CROYDON - BOXHILL AND ASSOCIATED LINES

August 2019

24B : to Weybridge & Surbiton

25 : to Surbiton

25 : to Leatherhead

WEST BYFLEET 21.54

EFFINGHAM JUNCTION 21.10

21.04

22.15

21.25

21.13

21.27

Amec Rail Plant

21.38 ON SDG

21.29

Effingham Down Sdg

GSP

HORSLEY 22.16

Controlled by Woking ASC (WK)

[SW 105] [BML 1] S : LSW (London & Southampton)

[SW 105] [BML 1] S : LSW (London & Southampton)

UP SLOW
UP FAST
DOWN FAST
DOWN SLOW

Platforms
1-4   12
5   12 Up 14 Down
6   6

Former Signal Box 'listed'
* Mileage calculation excludes Up Bay Platform 3

25.65

24.00

23.70

East End Sdg

WOKING 24.27*

24.06

24.14

24.18

ASC (WK) 24.20

CLANDON 25.26

[SW 200] [NGL] S : LSW

GSP 25.20

UP COBHAM
DOWN COBHAM

Merrow 26.61

Miles from Waterloo via Cobham

Woking Up Yard

[WKG 9]

25.013

No.2 UP SDG

No.1 REC

24.76

DEAD END

DEAD END

No.2 RECEPTION

No.1 RECEPTION

25.12

25.05

Woking Jn

24.56

24.40

24.30

24.24

24.62

HURDLES RD

SN

BOTTOM YD

BOTTOM SHED

TOP KHYBER

TOP K

KHYBER

CROOK

BRIDGE

MIDDLE BLOCK

CRANE

Day Aggregates

Balfour Beatty ★

Redland Aggregates

Woking Down Yard

[WKG 8]

Woking Up Yard

Miles from Waterloo
(Mileage variations exist between
Waterloo and Southampton/Exeter)

UP SLOW
UP FAST
DOWN FAST
DOWN SLOW

25.00

25.09

UP GUILDFORD

DOWN GUILDFORD

(WK) 26.34 (GD)

R. Bourne

WORPLESDON 26.55

[SW 110] [WPH 1] S : LSW

(WK) (GD) 27.62

LONDON ROAD
(Guildford) 28.47

Guildford New Line Jn

29.50 Guildford North Jn

Carriage Sdgs

29.23

29.26

30 (via Woking)

30.20 [Woking end   Platforms 3-8
         Cobham end   Platforms 2-8

GTW1   WPH1   NGL
30.35   30.05

(a) ASH   30.07   29.52
(b) COBHAM 30.14   29.59
(c) MAIN

GUILDFORD 30.27

* 30.20 (via Woking; mileage reversal at 30.20 to [GTW])

29.70 (via Cobham)

ASC 30.40

Platforms 2-8 designated
London End
Portsmouth End/South End

Platforms 1,2,3,4,5,6,8 a (not 7)
Lines reversible except Platforms 2 & 4

River Wey Vdct

North Box Sdgs

PERTURBATION

29.65

UP MAIN 30.02

DOWN MAIN 29.77

UP ASH

DN ASH

29.28

Chalk Tunnel (845 yds)

(GD) ASC 30.43

UP MAIN
DN MAIN

UP SDG

30.26

Carriage Sdgs 30.20

[SW 110] [WPH 1] S : LSW

= Servicing Platform

Platforms
1   10
2   8 Up 12 Down
3-7
8   10

* = 3 way point

BROOKWOOD 27.79

27.63

28.12

GSP 28.10

Pirbright Jn (29.39 mean)

29½

29.31

29.51

29.60

UP ALTON
DOWN ALTON

[SW 120] [PAA 1] S : LSW

WANBOROUGH 34.29

UP ASH
DOWN ASH

A3 31.20

A3 31.20

ASH 49.18

(former Ash Jn)

[COM] S : SE S : LSW
48.34 35.50

[SW 265] [GTW 1]

Miles from Waterloo
via Worplesdon & Guildford (reverse)
at 30.20 (WPH 1)

(CCTV&GD) 49.15

Aldershot South Jn 50.01

[SW 265] [GTW 2] S : SE

UP BLACKWATER
DN BRANCH

[SW 120] [SW 265] [NSA] S : LSW

0.00

27C : to Farnborough

27C : to Aldershot

27C : to Aldershot

27C : to North Camp

Miles from Charing Cross via Redhill

27A & 29A : to Haslemere, Dorking & Redhill

Controlled by Guildford ASC (GD)

Miles from Waterloo between

August 2019

© Copyright TRACKmaps. No reproduction without permission

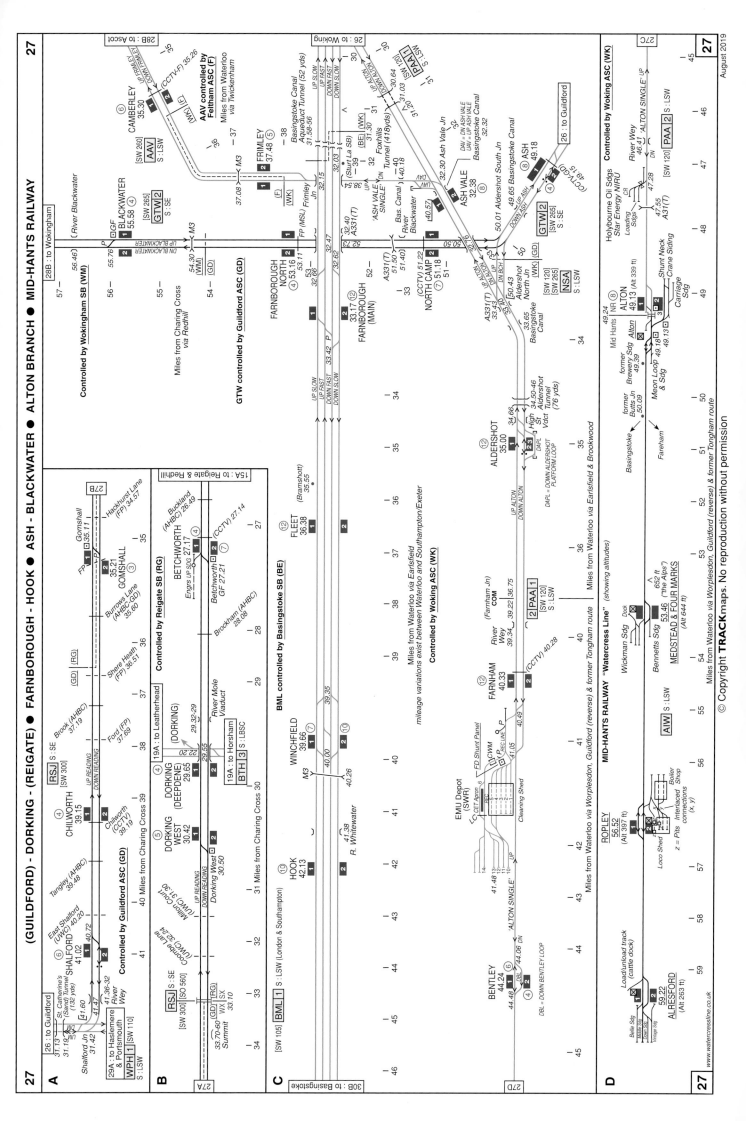

FELTHAM – READING ● WINDSOR BRANCH ● CHERTSEY BRANCH

A

22 : to Richmond & Waterloo

22 : to Willesden & Waterloo

[SW 210] [SW 230] HJW   13.39

HOUNSLOW

Whitton Jn   13.03

Hounslow Jn   14.09

[SW 230] HOU S:LSW   14.38

Feltham Jn   13.35

River Crane 13.77   DOWN MAIN

Feltham Depot (SWR) (Proposed)

CET apron

ASC(F) 14.60

Longford River 14.70

14.68   FELTHAM

[SW 210] RDG1 S:LSW

= UP/DOWN ARRIVALS

Oakmead (UWC) 18.30

East Yard

Staines West Jn   EMU Berthing Sdgs   18.47

Staines East Jn 19.44

ASHFORD (Middx) 17.40

(Planned closure, to be replaced by Feltham – see right)

River Colne 19.48

Staines East Sdg 19.52

River Colne 19.59

STAINES 19.02

Staines Bridge (R. Thames) 19.26

[SW 210] RDG1 S:LSW

Thorpe Lane (CCTV) 19.67

20.40 M25 Bridges

River Colne 20.16

Wraysbury River 19.59

#

SWX (OOU)

Former Oil Depot 19.40

Pooley Green (CCTV) 20.51

EGHAM (CCTV) 21.08   21.02

20.60 M25

Rusham (AHBC) 21.61

[SW 250] SWE S:LSW

WRAYSBURY 21.40

SUNNYMEADS 22.48

Controlled by Feltham ASC (F)

Miles from Waterloo via Twickenham

Black Potts Vdct (R. Thames) 24.74 24.63

DATCHET 23.63 / 23.69

Mays (CCTV) 23.74

[SW 210] RDG1 S:LSW

LONGCROSS 25.11

WINDSOR & ETON RIVERSIDE 25.48

25.23

SUNNINGDALE 26.71

London Road (CCTV) 26.66

Miles from Waterloo via Twickenham

UP WINDSOR / DOWN WINDSOR

VIRGINIA WATER 23.15 / 23.06   23.01

24.74 / 24.65 / 24.24 / 24.20 / 24.14

Lyne Bridge (M25) (Rail suspension bridge)

UP CHERTSEY / DOWN CHERTSEY

23.37

CHERTSEY 22.25

[SW 255] VWW S:LSW

(CCTV) 22.20

ADDLESTONE 20.71

20.25 River Wey Navigation

20.06 River Wey

Bourne 20.56 / 20.65

River 19.74 Addlestone Jn

-0.02

(WK) Woking (CCTV-WK)

[SW 255] AJB

24B : to Woking

24B : to Weybridge

Miles from Waterloo via Weybridge

B

EARLEY 66.01 / 66.04

(T) (WM)

[SW 210] RDG2 S:SE

WINNERSH 64.10

WINNERSH TRIANGLE 64.72

River Loddon 65.16

WOKINGHAM 62.08 / 62.03

COM 61.72 / 62.01   56.35

Wokingham Jn

(WM) 62.60

R. Emmbrook

M4 63.42

Miles from Charing Cross via Redhill

Emmbrook River 61.49

UP GUILDFORD / DOWN GUILDFORD

61.59

CROWTHORNE 58.66

[SW 265] GTW2 S:SE   Controlled by Wokingham (WM)

SANDHURST 57.22

27C : to Blackwater

27C : to Camberley

BAGSHOT 32.08   33.60 / 33.66

[SW 260] AAV S:LSW

Jenkins Hill (UWC) 33.23

Bagshot Tunnel (121 yds)

Guildford Road Viaduct 32.26-28

UP FRIMLEY / DOWN FRIMLEY

Controlled by Wokingham (WM)

MARTINS HERON 31.09

[SW 210] RDG1 S:LSW

(F) 31.20 (WM)

BRACKNELL 32.24

Englemere (UWC) 29.36

A329(M) 34.07

Waterloo (AHBC) 34.76

Star Lane 35.30

Smiths (UWC) 35.73

ASCOT 28.79 / 29.04 / 29.18 / 29.28

[SW 210] RDG1 S:LSW   28.52 / 28.66

Controlled by Feltham ASC (F)

Miles from Waterloo via Twickenham

DOWN MAIN / UP MAIN (Ascot West) 30.03

Miles from Waterloo via Twickenham

Miles from Charing Cross via Redhill

28A

C

Controlled by Thames Valley Signalling Centre (TVSC)(T) (incl. Southern Lines from Earley)

Reading East Jn 35.61 / 35.40

Reading New Jn 35.40

GW MLN1 [GW 103]

UP RELIEF / DN RELIEF

UP MAIN / DN MAIN 35.40

RNJ [GW 190]

RLL [GW 195]

a = WR/WX 35.35

Vastern Road 35.64

[SW 210] RDG2 S:SE

READING 68.68 (Charing Cross)

WR/WX

UP SOUTHERN / DOWN SOUTHERN

RNJ Reading Spur Jn 68.35

Reading Southern Jn 67.74

R. Kennet 67.76

UP READING SPUR / DN READING SPUR 68.00

68.25 / 68.40

Book 3: to Maidenhead and Paddington

Miles from Charing Cross via Redhill

4,5,6   30A & Book 3:

28B

August 2019

© Copyright **TRACK**maps. No reproduction without permission

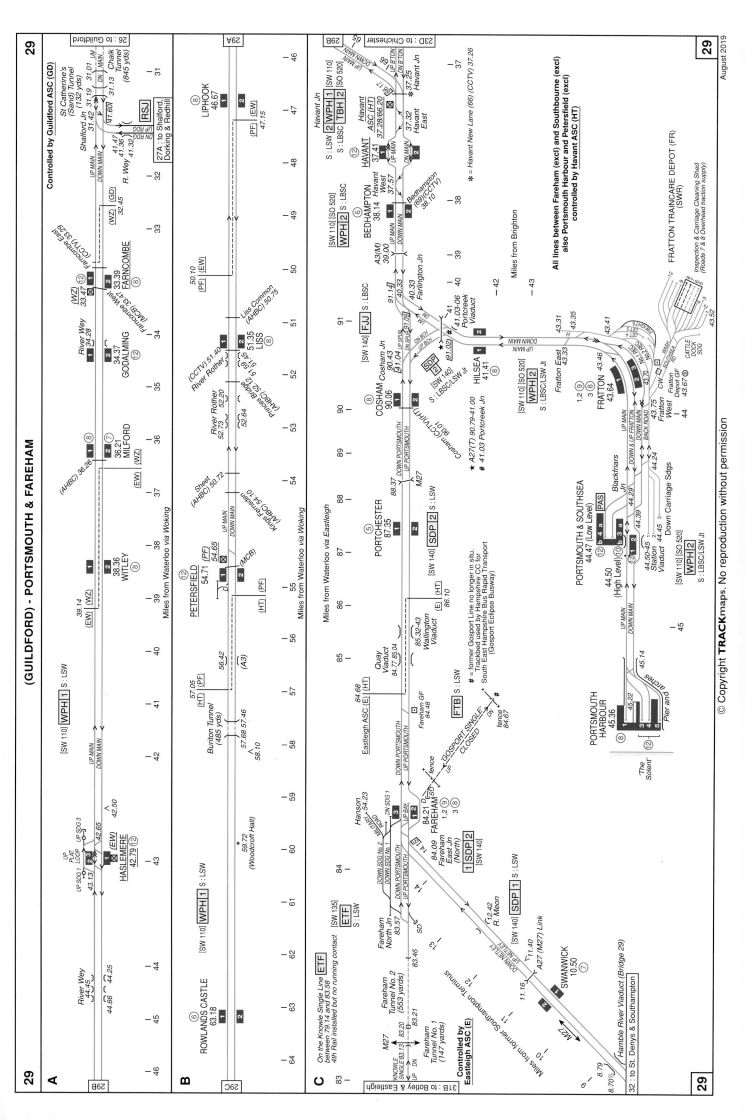

READING - BASINGSTOKE - WINCHESTER - SHAWFORD

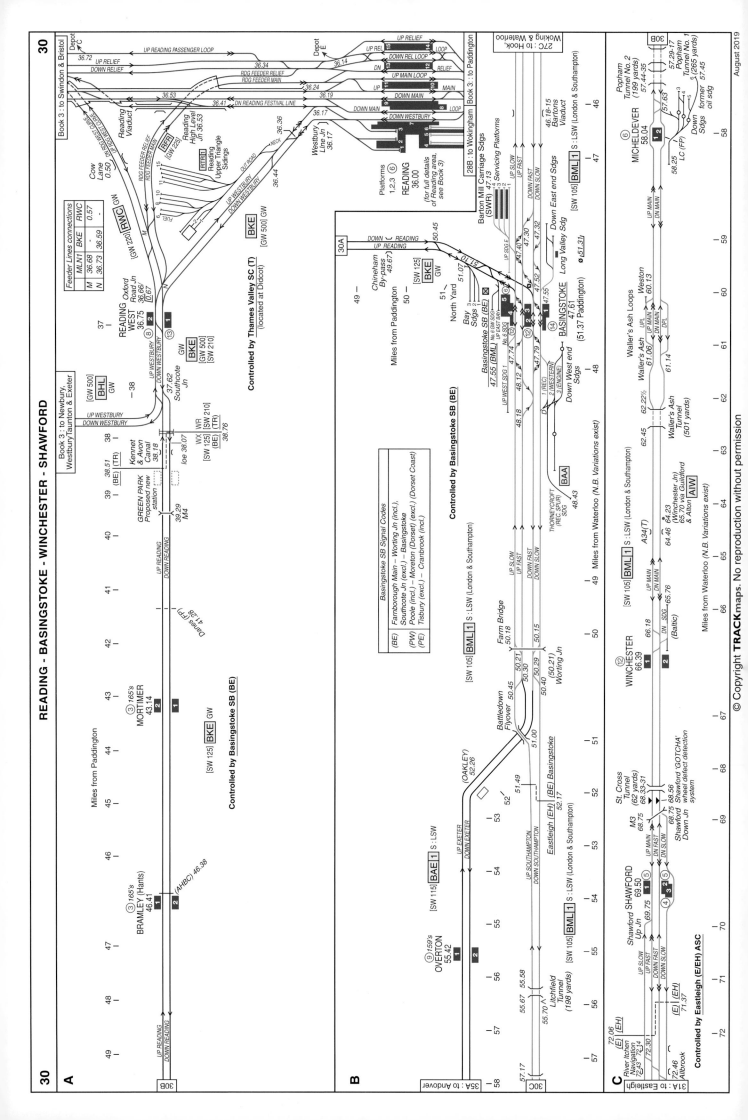

August 2019

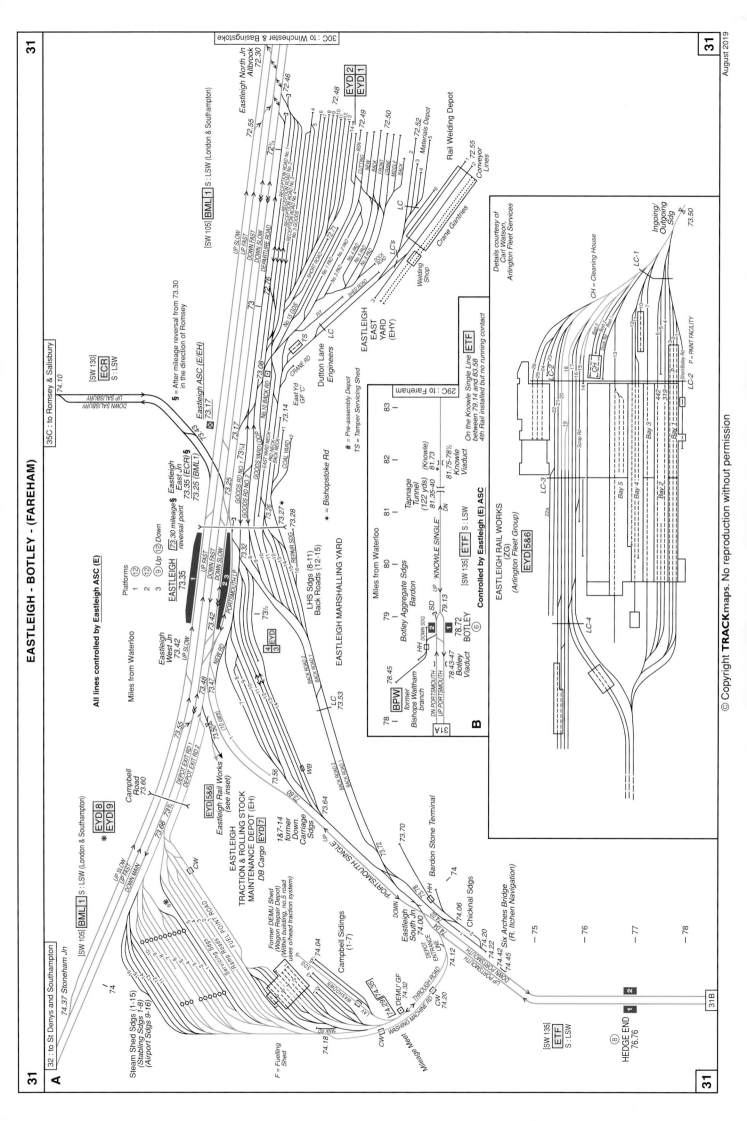

EASTLEIGH - BOTLEY - (FAREHAM)

August 2019

SOUTHAMPTON

A

Miles from Waterloo

−74

−75

−76

31A : to Eastleigh

Miniature railway •
see left

SOUTHAMPTON AIRPORT ⑫ (PARKWAY) 74.66

Stoneham Jn 74.37

M27 75.08

SWAYTHLING ④ 75.56

75.30 Swaything RAILBAM
(Rail Bearing Acoustic Monitor)

A3055 76.71

Adelaide Road (CCTV) 77.69

Itchen River Bridge (2)
2.17–23

Plat 2 ⑥
Plats 1,3,4 ⑦

ST. DENYS
77.10

St. Denys Jn

[SW 105] BML 1 S : LSW (London & Soton)

[SW 105] BML 2 S : LSW (Southampton & Dorchester)

Southampton Up Yard
(Bevois Park Sidings)

1 = No. 1 RECEP
2 = No. 2 RECEP

former
Breedon, Southampton
Concrete Plant

77.15

77.02
−77

77.25/1.45

77.30

Sea Wall

Main
Traincare
Facility
(OTS)

CET
Discharge

77.35

NK

UP FAST
UP SLOW
DOWN SLOW
DOWN FAST

77.54
Gantry
77.68 #

77.44

Northam Jn
78.01

77.58

77.68 # COM (Northam Short Mile)
78.00 (Northam)

Mount Pleasant
(CCTV) 77.54

WASHER
No. 1 REC
No. 2 REC
SHED NK

NORTHAM ARR/DEP 78.24

SDG 8
SDG A

78.17

Servicing
platforms

6 7 8 9
6 7 8 9

NORTHAM Md DEP 78.24

SHUNTING NECK
CW 78.17 Northam Rd Bridge
78.20 (Northam)

Northam Traincare Facility (NT)
SWR /Siemens Transportation Systems Ltd (STSL)
Shed 213m (10 x 20m or 9 x 23m coaches) - OTS = overhead
traction supply Track 4 - bogie drop pit
WL - Wheel Lathe BL - Battery loco

BML 1
BML 2

78.76

78.37

78.43

Southampton
Tunnel
(528 yds)

SOUTHAMPTON
CENTRAL ⑬

79.19

79.37

UP GOODS LOOP
UP FAST
UP SLOW
DOWN SLOW
DOWN FAST
DN LP EXT.
DN LOOP

79.68
79.55
79.78

4th
rail
elec

UM 78.28½ −18
DM 78.28½ −17

79

Miles from Waterloo
(NB variations exist)

Associated
British Ports

Town Quay

Mayflower
Cruise
Terminal

Mountbatten
Way
79.78

Ramps

LC (P & O)

80
Concrete
apron

Container
handling area

SOUTHAMPTON
WESTERN DOCKS

Berkeley Jn

(104–101
Berths)

105 81.27
Terminal shed

105
Berth

106
Berth

107
Berth

107
shed

Gypsum
handling
area

Stone
loading
pad

108
Berth

109
Berth

MILLBROOK ⑧
80.11

1 2

MILLBROOK
FREIGHTLINER
TERMINAL
(SZ)

Crane area

UP FAST CR
UP SLOW
DOWN SLOW
DOWN FAST
DN DOCKS BCH
UP DOCKS BCH

80.15 DN DOCKS BCH
80.27

No. 12
Gate Mlk Dk Ent/Exit

Ansa Logistics
Terminal

[SW 147] MIS

West Bay Road
(TMO)

NR
ABP

80.32

Church
Lane

RB GD = REDBRIDGE GOODS

RB GD
80.45
MARITIME BACK ROAD
80.52

UP MAIN
DOWN MAIN
80.70

33A : to Redbridge

CR

SOY S : LSW (London & Southampton)
[SW 145]

EASTERN DOCKS SINGLE

Carnaby
Rd
(AOCL)
79.20

Maritime Way
Central Road
(TMO)

LC

Ocean
Dock

NR
ABP
79.04

No. 3 Rail Gate

79.00

41 Berth Shed

Queen Elizabeth II Terminal
(38/39 berth)

79.74

SOUTHAMPTON
EASTERN DOCKS

Empress
Dock

River
Itchen

RIVER TEST

B

MONKS BROOK HALT

LC LC

www.steamtrain.co.uk

Top curve

South
LC

Traverser

Workshop

7¼"
only

Loading
Ramp

1 2 3

EASTLEIGH PARKWAY

[SW 105] BML 2

LC

Lakeside
Tunnel

Lakes

LC LC

EASTLEIGH LAKESIDE RAILWAY
Dual 7¼" & 10½" gauge   2100 yards

Miniature railway •
see left

C   EXBURY GARDENS RAILWAY, Beaulieu
12¼" gauge, about 1¼ miles of track

Dragonfly Halt
(Not in public use)

EXBURY
NORTH

LC LC LC LC

Viaduct

Dragonfly Pond

Tunnel

Summer Lane Pond

(NFRU)

Carriage
Shed &
Exhibition

Loco
Shed

EXBURY
CENTRAL

Details courtesy of P. Scott

BURSLEDON ⑧
8.49

2 1

29C : to Fareham

HAMBLE ④
7.19

2 1

Hamble Rd (TMOB)

Hamble Rd (open)

(OOU)

former
BP Oil Ltd

NETLEY ⑧
6.45

2 1

GF 'B' 6.42

SHOLING ⑧
4.58

2 1

[SW 140] SDP 1 S : LSW

Miles from former Southampton Terminus

8

7

6

5

4

−3

BITTERNE ⑥
2.36

2 1

GF 'E' 4.21

WOOLSTON ⑦
4.11

Miles from former Southampton Terminus

DOWN NETLEY
UP NETLEY

77.68 COM (Northam Short Mile)
78.00 (Northam)

Miniature railway •
see below

All lines controlled by Eastleigh ASC (E)

D   ROYAL VICTORIA RAILWAY, Netley
10¼" gauge   About 2½ miles of track

A

KIRK
TERMINUS
(not yet open)

LC LS1

LC

Carriage Shed

Pit

Loco Sheds

LC PICCADILLY

LC CHAPEL ROAD B

LS = Loading Spur
A - B Trackbed of former standard gauge Hospital branch from Netley, closed '55

www.royalvictoriarailway.co.uk

Details courtesy of P. Scott

August 2019

© Copyright TRACKmaps. No reproduction without permission

(SOUTHAMPTON) - TOTTON - SWAY ● FAWLEY BRANCH ● LYMINGTON BRANCH

A

Controlled by Brockenhurst SB (BH)

Controlled by Eastleigh ASC (E)

32: to Southampton

b = Maritime East Jn 80.70

S : LSW (Southampton & Dorchester) [SW 105] BML 2

80.70
Crane area
(20 flats)
Wagon repair sdgs 81.00
Wagon storage sdgs 81.06
81
Loco Servicing Pt 81.42
Repair Shop

MARITIME FREIGHTLINER TERMINAL (SZ)

35C : to Romsey and Salisbury

[SW 150] RTJ 1 S : LSW
Redbridge Jn (7) REDBRIDGE 81.70 1
GF 'B' LD 81.69
Depot Reception Sdgs
81.76 2

UP TEST VALLEY 23.13
DOWN 23.13½
UP MAIN DOWN MAIN

Future Terminal layout – late 2020

DOWN MAIN
2 a
LD Depot Reception Sdgs
GF 'B' LD 81.69 Repair Shop BS

RD GD = REDBRIDGE GOODS
BS = BEHIND THE SHED ROAD
LD = LOADING DOCK SDG
a = Maritime West Jn 81.40

Ø = 82.08 - 82.06½ Redbridge Channel Bridge

R. Test Bridge 82.06½
R. Test Bridge 82.43
TOTTON 82.43
(7) Totton (Junction Rd) (CCTV) 82.55
1 2

Fawley Branch Jn, Totton Jn East 82.67
FAWLEY
GDS LP
Down Sdgs SD
Totton Jn West
83.24 83.30 83.33
Bartley Water 83.39
Ashurst Stream 83.61

FAWLEY SINGLE UP DN

Jacob's Gutter Lane (UWC) 84.12
White's (UWC) 85.00
Trotts Lane (AHBC) 85.11

Tavell's Lane (AHBC) 85.66
(MGH) 86.06 MULBERRY HALT Pfm
(MW) MARCHWOOD 86.10
MGH 86.23
Pumpfield Farm (MSL) 86.37
(86.40) Reception & Exchange Sdgs

McGee No. 2 (UWC) 86.61
Veal's Lane (AHBC) 86.69
McGee No. 3 (UWC) 86.78
McGee No. 4 (UWC) 87.02
Church Farm No. 1 (UWC)(NT) 87.14
Church Farm No. 2 (UWC)(NT) 87.37

West Street (AHBC) 88.38
School Road (MGH) 88.68

Robert's Camp Transport Sdgs (86.75)

RIVER TEST

Mulberry Jetty
Falklands Jetty
JETTY Pfm
PORT GATE Pfm
Regulating Sdgs
Loading Sdgs
South Sdgs ¥
¥ = South Sdgs
Loco Shed

DSDA MARCHWOOD MILITARY PORT
Ministry of Defence

FAWLEY SINGLE UP DN
Frost Lane (AHBC) 89.60
HYTHE 89.31
(Hardley) 90.12½
Developing Co. No. 5 (UWC)(NT) 90.47
Developing Co. No. 2 90.62
Developing Co. No. 3 (UWC)(NT) 90.32½

HYTHE PIER RAILWAY
2 foot gauge, 240v dc 3rd rail
29 chains
Pier
Southampton Water

= Fawley GF 'C' 91.42
(OOU)
NR Esso 91½
Cadland Quay Cottage (UWB) 91.33
91
(OOU) 92

CADLANDS
Block 50 LPG Loading
Esso
MAIN LINE
Cadland (E Ave) 91.69
BR DN REC 2
BR DN REC 1
BR 1 2 3
TR 1 2 3 4 5 6 7 8 9 10 11
TRIO
Cripple Sdgs
Bombardier
'K' Spur
Crude off loading
(NIRU)

TOP SITE

Chlorine Facilities
ZONE 2 (AGW1)
Esso (Anglo Gulf & West Indies)
Loco Shed
WB Bitumen
Gas oil
A
TR 1 TR 2
SWAMP RD
MIDDLE RD FAWLEY 92.12
PLATFM RD 92.10
SHED RD Depot 2
COAL RD

FAWLEY REFINERY
Esso (ExxonMobil)

Block 9 - Caustic Facilities
CMB
Chemical Facilities
Blending
Chlorine Facilities
Butyl Rubber

RUNNING ROAD
D'ARDYNE

August 2019

© Copyright **TRACKmaps**. No reproduction without permission

B

[SW 105] BML 2 S : LSW (Southampton & Dorchester)

ASHURST NEW FOREST
85.34 (8) 1 2

(5) **BEAULIEU ROAD** 88.06 1 2

89.40 (E)
(BH) (E)

SWAY 95.45 (7) 1 2

Miles from Waterloo

Lymington River 92.13

(BC) (BH)
Bournemouth 97.06

33A

[SW 105] BML 2 S : LSW

Lymington Rd (McB) 92.55
Luggage Platform GF 92.62 (12)
UP SDG
DN PASS LP 93.05
DN SDG 93.15
ENGRS SDG
93.25
Brockenhurst Jn
(Lymington Jn) 93.60

(BH) 92.57
BROCKENHURST 92.66
a 3 4 b
UP L (13)

LYMINGTON SINGLE UP DN

95.32 (Shirley Holmes)
96.61
AMPRESS WORKS (private, closed)
Lymington Town (CCTV) 97.48
97.64-67 Lymington Viaduct
Sea wall 97.67
97.04

[SW 160] BLP S : LSW
LYMINGTON TOWN 97.57 (4)
LYMINGTON PIER 98.15 (8)
Lymington Pier (UWC) 98.05
98.15

Miles from Waterloo

34A : to Bournemouth

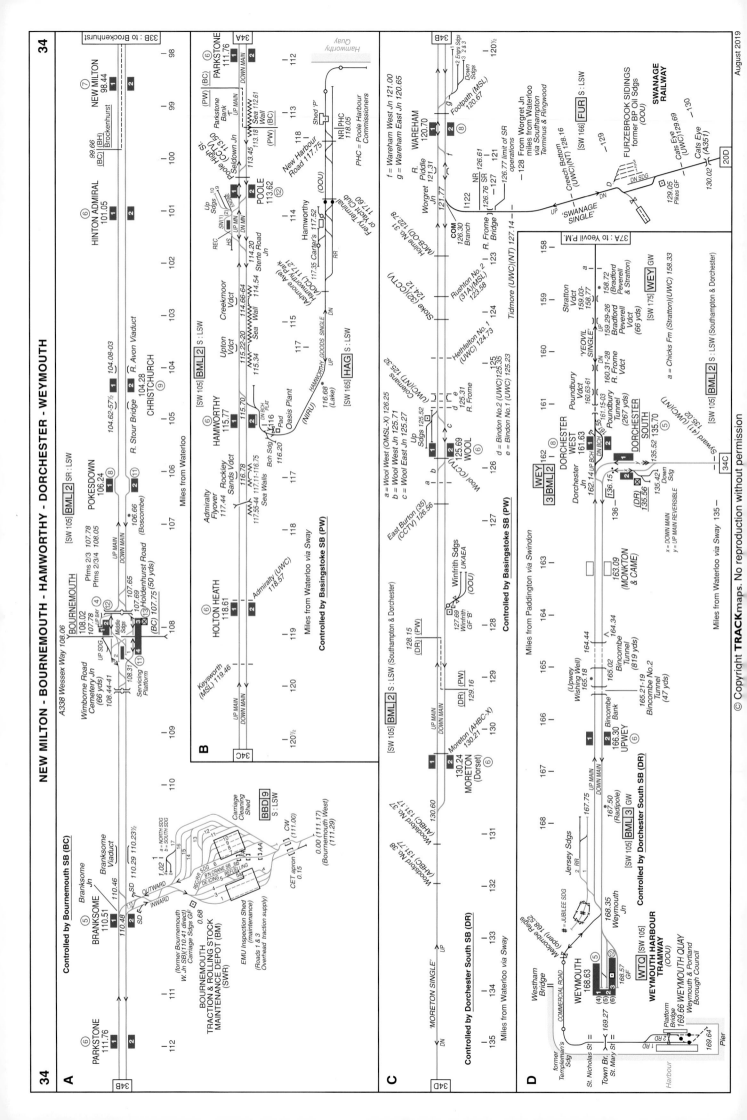

NEW MILTON - BOURNEMOUTH - HAMWORTHY - DORCHESTER - WEYMOUTH

34

August 2019

© Copyright TRACKmaps. No reproduction without permission

WHITCHURCH - SALISBURY ● LUDGERSHALL BRANCH ● SALISBURY - ROMSEY - EASTLEIGH and REDBRIDGE

A

30B : to Basingstoke

⑨ 159s
WHITCHURCH (Hants) 59.08
A34(T)
59.36 59.15
Former Didcot, Newbury
& Southampton Rly

Hurstbourne
Viaduct
61.18-11

62.47

UP EXETER
DOWN EXETER

Controlled by **Basingstoke SB (BE)**

[SW 115] BAE 1 S : LSW

ANDOVER 66.19
⑨ 159s
Up Yard — D

Andover Lane
(UWC)(NT) 4.50
— 5
— 4
— 3

66.54
UP
66.27
BRANCH
UP EXETER
DOWN EXETER
Andover GF

M & SW Jn
Ludgershall Jn
[SW 115]
LUD 2 (LUDGERSHALL)
LUD 1

Phil Hill Brook
or
Monxton
Viaduct
68.42-38

1.71 ● (Weyhill)
1.52 (A303(T)
0.00 (Red Post Jn)
67.61
67.16
A303(T)
2
DN

Dock 6.08
6 Ptm
5.71 ● 5.61
5.64
Horse
Sdgs
WDNR
6.15
Perham
Jn
Shed
Shed
CY
6.42

DSDA LUDGERSHALL
Ministry of Defence (Army)

⑨ 159s
GRATELEY 72.49
1
2 (BE) Basingstoke
(SY) LSW
73.20 72.57
73.25

UP EXETER
DOWN EXETER

Miles from Waterloo

B

35A

[SW 115] BAE 1 (BE) Basingstoke

(Idmiston) 77.38
78.00
Targets (UWC) 78.21
(SY)
78.07 (Porton)

[SW 115] BAE 1 S : LSW

Laverstock North Jn 82.05
Salisbury
Tunnel Jn 82.36
Fisherton
Tunnel (443 yds)
A36(T) 82.63
82.57
83.06
NK
LAVERSTOCK LOOP [SW 115 & 150]
82.11 82.39
95.61
Laverstock
South Jn
UP DEAN

East
Grimstead
90.10
East
Grimstead

UP DEAN
92.05 (Alderbury Jn)
92.75

Sir Frederick's Bridge or
Milford
Clarendon Park
Curve
Viaduct
93.67

LAV BR (LSW)

[SW 150] RTJ 2 S : LSW

Controlled by **Salisbury SB (SY)**

Miles from Waterloo via Andover

Maintenance Shed
Berthing
Sdgs
83.47 ENGRS
THRO SDG
ENGRS
Salisbury
East Sdgs
UP MAIN
DOWN MAIN
DN SDG 1
DN SDG 2
East Carriage
Holding Sdgs
83.00
83.28
83.43 (SY)

ARR/DEP
UP MAIN
DOWN MAIN

SALISBURY TRAINCARE DEPOT (SWR)
DEPOT REC
PLATFORM
DEPOT REC
NR Salisbury
Delivery
Unit

SALISBURY 83.43

Platforms
2&3 12
4 14
6 7

SAL GW
COM
84.00 83.72
'Fisherton Short Mile'
84.35
83.63
2 BAE 1

CET
DEP
SDG
CW2 CW1

36A : to Swindon

Miles from Paddington
via Swindon

[SW 170]
Quidhampton:(Tinkerpit)
Broadlands Quarry (closed)
Imerys Minerals Ltd
132.54
WILTON 132—
Wilton N. Jn
86.11
GF 132.25
UP MAIN
DOWN MAIN
84.36
A36(T)
(Skew
Bridge)
85.14

DN WESTBURY
UP WESTBURY

Wilton
Sth Jn
86.18
86.25
A36(T)

132.33
85.37
Wilton Jn

[SW 115] BAE 2 S : LSW (Salisbury & Yeovil)

3GB : to Tisbury & Yeovil Jn

35B

C

Eastleigh
ASC (E/EH)
73.17
⊠
BML 1
Eastleigh
East Jn
73.35
73.30
73.25

31A : to Basingstoke

M3 74.46
74.10 UP SALISBURY
DN SALISBURY
CHANDLER'S FORD
75.25 75

⊠ 1
④
BML 2

31A : to Eastleigh

23.3 ⊡
23.17
23.02
23.13
33A : to Southampton
81.76 Redbridge Jn
33A : to Totton

Chandlers (UWC)

Barks (UWC)
22
Nursling
21.51
M27 21.42
Miles from Andover Jn via former Stockbridge line

ECR SR : LSW
'SALISBURY SINGLE'
[SW 130]
DN
UP
[SW 150] RTJ 1 S : LSW

Controlled by **Eastleigh ASC (E)**

Miles from Andover Jn via Eastleigh (reverse)

Halterworth (AHBC) 79.24
79.68
79.24
ROMSEY
80.47
80.35
80.50
Romsey GF
18.16
ECR
2 RTJ 1
2 6 ⑦
1

UP SALISBURY
DOWN SALISBURY
DN SALIS
UP SALIS
UP TEST VALLEY
DOWN TEST VALLEY

Test River
Bridge (20)
81.18
(SY) (E)
(E)

MOTTISFONT
& DUNBRIDGE
(formerly DUNBRIDGE)
84.21
R. Dun 85.19
Dunbridge (UWC) 84.31
Kimbridge (AHBC-X) 84.24
1 2
3
Trusions (UWC) 83.05
Bullet's (UWC) 82.60
Terry's (UWC) 82.30

Controlled by **Salisbury SB (SY)**

Dean Hill (MCB-OD) 86.57
(SY) (E)
UP DEAN
DOWN DEAN

Bishops (UWC) 86.73
R. Dun 87.47
DEAN 88.10
R. Dun 88.15
(MCB-OD) 88.14
[SW 150] RTJ 2 S : LSW
⑦
2 D
1

Miles from Waterloo via Eastleigh (reverse)

35B

35C

Miles from Waterloo via Andover

35

August 2019

© Copyright **TRACKmaps**. No reproduction without permission

A

Book 3: to Westbury

3B : to Salisbury

Controlled by Westbury ASC (W)

Controlled by Salisbury SB (SY)

Coulston Bottom (UWC) 130.16
R. Wylye 131.15 / 131.31
131.53 (Wilton North)
129.12 (Wishford)

Wyle College Road (UWC) 125.38
Eton Road (UWC) 125.38
Hindon Road (UWC) 124.41
Wylye (AHBC) 124.12
Townsend (UWC) 123.36
Wylye GF 'B' 124.38
125.12 (Langford)

Middle Road (UWC) 122.36
A303
Stockton (MSL-X) 122.40
Tytning (MSL) 122.75
123.79 A303

Sherrington (UWC) 121.02
Sherrington Viaduct 121.26-29
[SW 170] SAL GW

Codford (AHBC) 120.45
Upton Lovell (AHBC) 119.70
119.62 R. Wylye

R. Wylye 117.77
Heytesbury 118.23
SAL [SW 170]
DOWN WESTBURY
UP WESTBURY

DSDA Beechgrove Sidings
Ministry of Defence (Army)
Beechgrove GF 'Z' 115.40
115.27
Westbury (W) 115.40
[GW 500] SW 170]

WARMINSTER 114.37
114.77
114.45
Warminster HABD 113.73
112.42 (Upton Scudamore)
DOWN SALISBURY
UP SALISBURY

DILTON MARSH 111.11 (mean)
Warminster Incline
114.14 / 114.07
Miles from Paddington via Swindon

B

3B : to Salisbury
Controlled by Salisbury SB (SY)

WILTON Wilton 86.11
86.18 A36(T)
Wilton Sth Jn 86.25

[SW 115] BAE 2 S : LSW (Salisbury & Yeovil)
'EXETER MAIN'
UP / DN

Barford St. Martin Viaduct 88.68

Hurdcott Lodge (MSL) 89.74
Morris Farm No. 2 (UWC) 90.35

DINTON 91.72
Baverstock Sdg
(OOU) (OOU)

Chilmark (MSL) 93.41
Teffont Mill (MSL) 92.39
CHILMARK SIDING
MOD
Swallowns (UWC) 93.21

Tisbury Quarry (MSL) 94.75
[SW 115] SAL
'EXETER MAIN'
TISBURY LOOP

TISBURY 96.14
Tisbury West (AHBC) 96.71
(3) 159's (4) 170's
96.00

Semley Summit 101.03
Semley Gates (BW) 100.24
101.13 SEMLEY

Lennaty (SE46)
119.15
(6) 159's

Sherborne (CCT) 118.00
Castleton (UWC) 117.31

118.04
SHERBORNE

Basingstoke (SE) (SY)
[SW 115] (SY)
BAE 2 S : LSW (Salisbury & Yeovil)
Miles from Waterloo via Andover

C

Controlled by Basingstoke SB (SE)

Hunts Path No. 2 (UWC) 103.92
Hunts Path No. 1 (UWC)

a = Gillingham West Jn 105.36
b = Gillingham East Jn 105.07
Gillingham Viaduct 106.30-28

GILLINGHAM 105.23
(6) 159's 105.24
Gillingham GF
UP SDG DN LOOP
2 1
105.46
DN SDG

Buckhorn Weston or Gillingham Tunnel (742 yds)
107.35 107.44 107.78
EXETER MAIN

Ashford (MSL) 109.41
Level 110.58 109.50

TEMPLECOMBE 112.02
112.08
Former Somerset & Dorset Rly
111.67
Down Sdg
(6) 159's

113.34
Milborne Port
114.31

Crewkerne Tunnel (205 yds) 132.48-39
CREWKERNE 131.33
Crewkerne (AHBC)
(SE65) 132.03
(6) 159's

[SW 115] BAE 2 S : LSW
UP / DOWN EXETER
DOWN EXETER
'EXETER MAIN'
Miles from Waterloo via Andover

Basingstoke (SE) (SY)

D

37A : to Yeovil Pen Mill & Castle Cary

'HEART OF WESSEX LINE'
WEY [SW 175]
Bedwin Farm No. 1 (UWC)
Wyke No. 2 (SE31) 120.60
Wyke No. 1 (UWC) 120.51
119.93 (SE48)

WEY : to Yeovil, Somerset & Weymouth
GWR : Wilts, Somerset & Weymouth
UP / DN EXETER
[SW 115] BAE 2 S : LSW
120
121
122.03 (Bradford Abbas Jn)
122.19

S : LSW
[SW 175/115] YJP
UP / DN
142.66 DN EXETER
122.57
LC Wilderness
143
37A : to Dorchester & Weymouth

# = Yeovil Jn 122.31/0.00
Y = Yeovil Jn Up Sdg GF 122.300.12

(6) 159's Gillingham West Jn 105.36
(9)

YEOVIL JUNCTION 122.48 (-0.14)
YEOVIL RAILWAY CENTRE
South West Main Line Steam Co.
Loco shed
(Plat 3 for visiting excursions)
70ft

UP SDG
DN MAIN SDG
DN P SDG
DN SDG 1
Yeovil Jn 122.31/0.00

Grove Farm No. 1 (UWC) 127.34
126.20
124.67 (Sutton Bingham)
127.73 (Hardington)
Miles from Waterloo via Andover

[SW 115] BAE 2 S : LSW
'EXETER MAIN'
UP / DN

Controlled by Basingstoke SB (SE)

E

36D : to Yeovil Jn

Marchwood (SE73) 138.78
CHARD JUNCTION 139.35
139.24
former St. Ivel (OOU) 139.48
Chard Jn Down Sdgs
139.64
UP EXETER LOOP
UP / DN EXETER

Broom (AHBC) (SE-79) 141.57
Axe (AHBC) 141.14
Axminster (SE-89)(CCT) 144.15
Axminster East Jn 143.23
UP / DN EXETER
SINGLE
EXETER

A35(T) 145.0
AXMINSTER 144.48
(6) 159's
Axminster West Jn 146.09
Symminster (SE-9) 145.51
Symmakes (SE-9) 145.18
Army 90(UWC) 145.0

ø = Right-hand running normally applies between Axminster East and Axminster West Jns.

SEATON JUNCTION 147.63

Black Sand Bridge A35(T) 150.13
[SW 115] BAE 2 S : LSW

Hewish (AHBC) (SE71) 134.04
Hay (SE73) (UWC) 136.35

Honiton Tunnel (467) 153½ (1345 yds)
Honiton Incline Box 151.47
Honiton Bank (1:80) 152.45-150.08
152.45
153.26

Controlled by Basingstoke SB (SE)
Miles from Waterloo via Andover

37C : to Yeovil Jn

August 2019

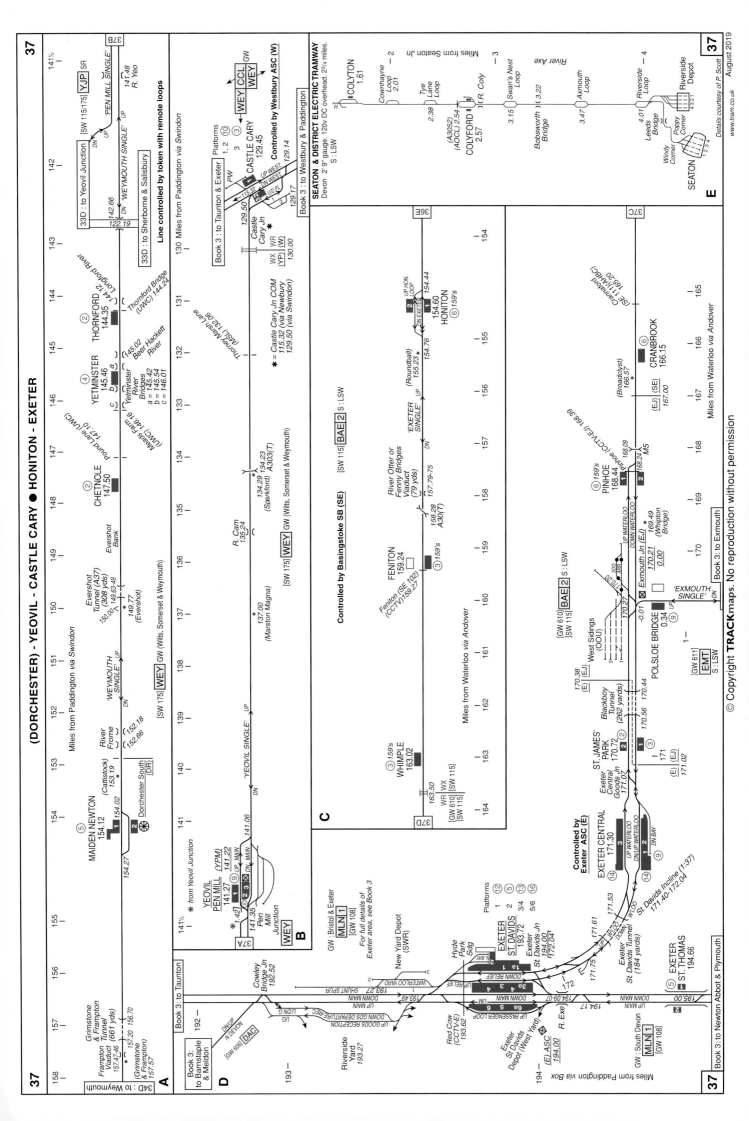

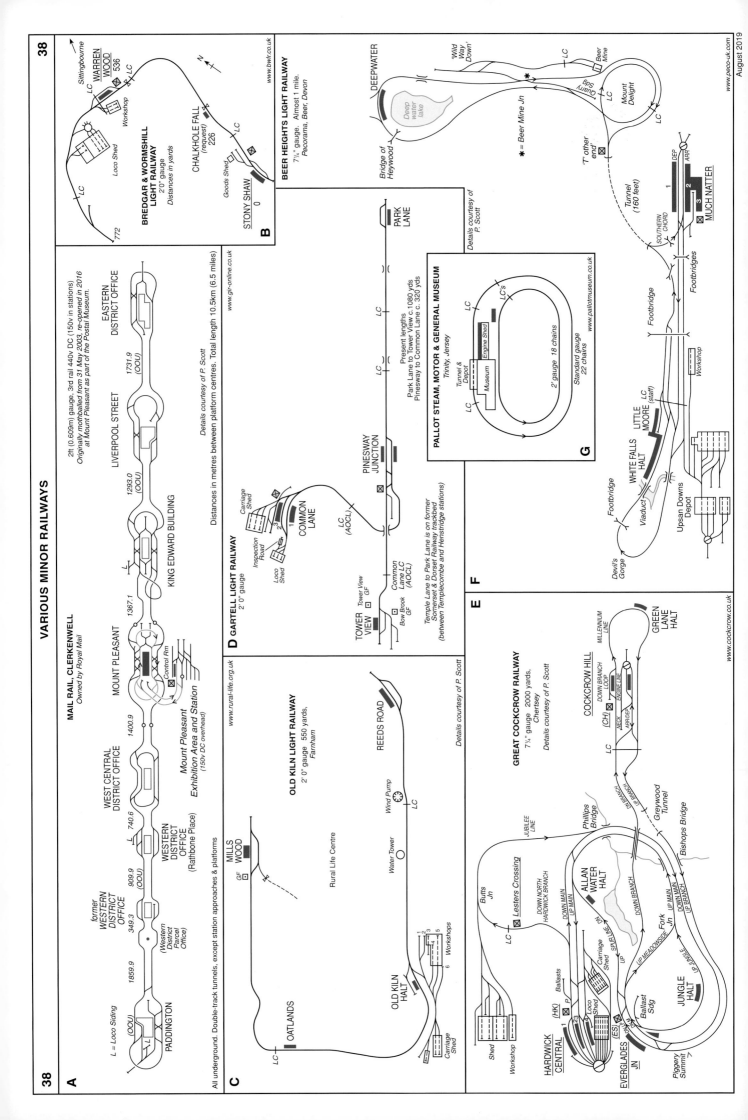

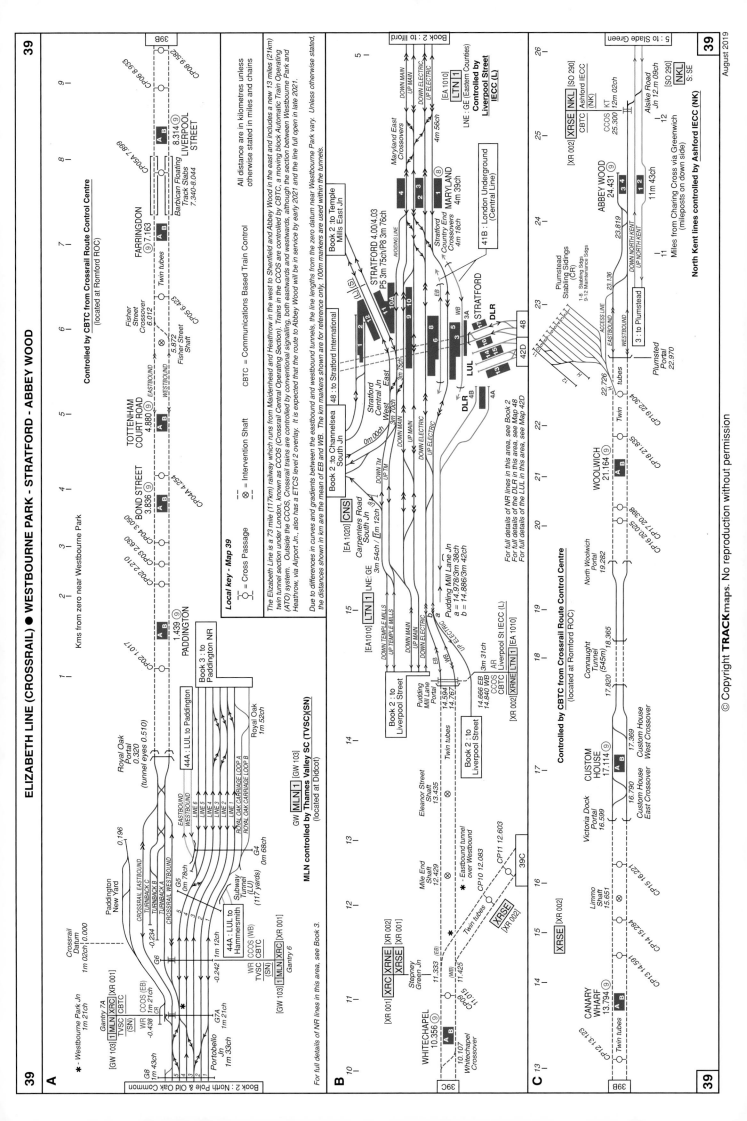

ELIZABETH LINE (CROSSRAIL) ● WESTBOURNE PARK - STRATFORD - ABBEY WOOD

Controlled by CBTC from Crossrail Route Control Centre
(located at Romford ROC)

All distance are in kilometres unless
otherwise stated in miles and chains

Local key - Map 39

○—○ = Cross Passage

⊗ = Intervention Shaft

CBTC = Communications Based Train Control

The Elizabeth Line is a 73 mile (117km) railway which runs from Maidenhead and Heathrow in the west to Shenfield and Abbey Wood in the east and includes a new 13 miles (21km) twin tunnel section under London, known as CCOS (Crossrail Central Operating Section). Trains in the CCOS are controlled by CBTC, a moving block Automatic Train Control (ATO) system. Outside the CCOS, Crossrail trains are controlled by conventional signalling, although the section between Westbourne Park and Heathrow, via Airport Jn., also has a ETCS level 2 overlay. It is expected that the route to Abbey Wood will be in service by early 2021 and the line full open in late 2021.

Due to differences in curves and gradients between the eastbound and westbound tunnels, the line lengths from the zero datum near Westbourne Park vary. Unless otherwise stated, the distances shown in km are the mean of EB and WB. The km markers are for reference only. 100m markers are used within the tunnels.

August 2019

© Copyright **TRACK**maps. No reproduction without permission

North Kent lines controlled by Ashford IECC (NK)

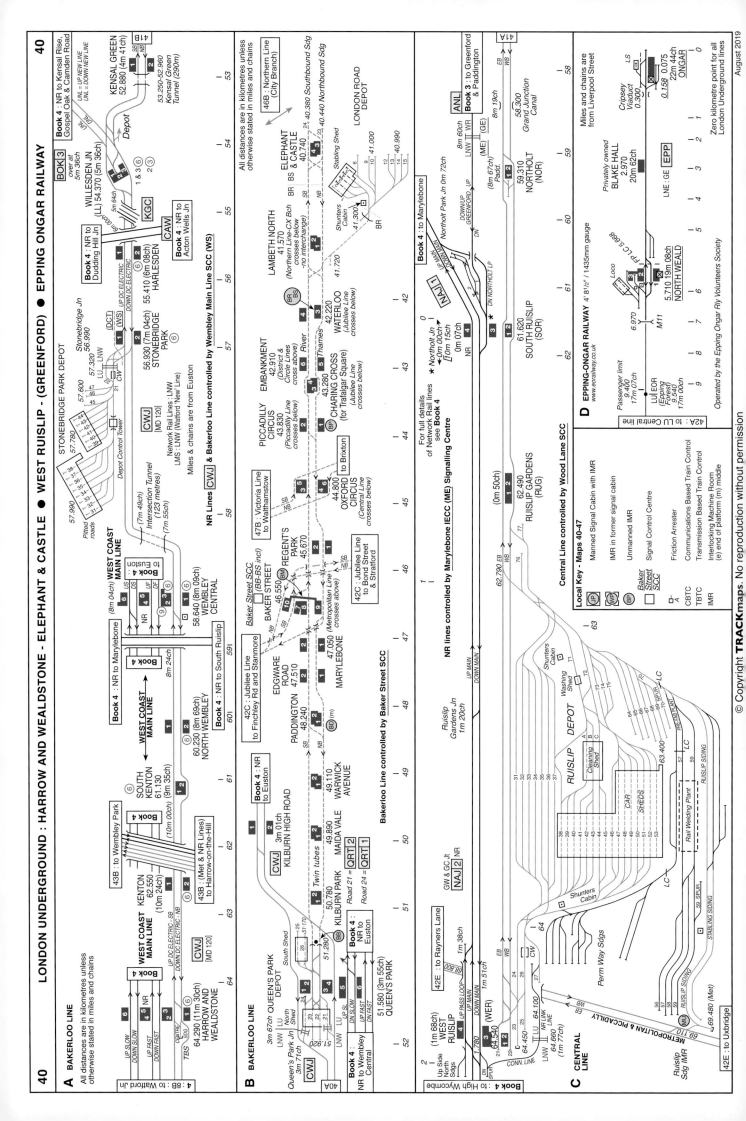

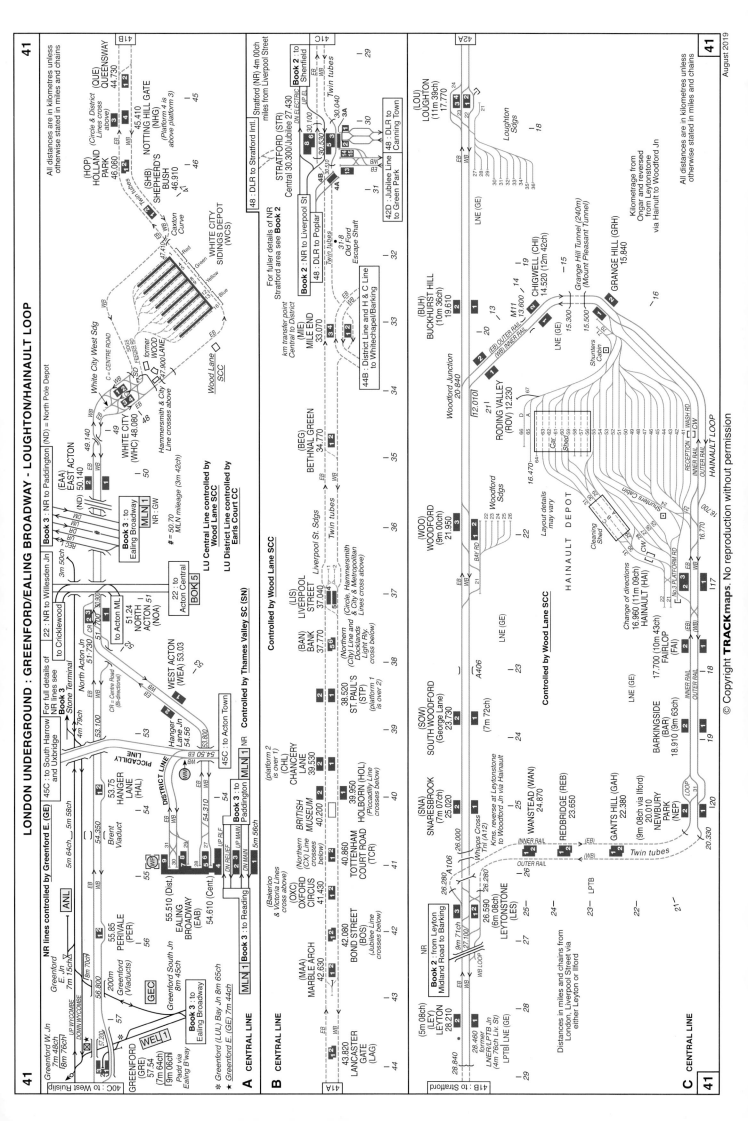

A CENTRAL LINE

Line controlled by Wood Lane SCC

All distances are in kilometres unless otherwise stated in miles and chains

43B

(DEB) DEBDEN 15.740 (12m 68ch)
22

SWISS COTTAGE
ST JOHN'S WOOD 48.610

(THB) THEYDON BOIS 12.390 (14m 73ch)
12.800

M25 11.100

(EPP) EPPING 9.850 (16m 39ch)
Break
LU | EOR 9.400 P. 9.510

LNE (GE)

40D : to Epping

B JUBILEE LINE

KINGSBURY 60.230
QUEENSBURY 61.560
CANONS PARK 63.270
STANMORE 64.620
(11m 19ch) Baker St (Met)

Stanmore Sidings
T = Tamping Machine Spur
SD
64.04
T

Stations Westminster to North Greenwich have platform edge doors

C JUBILEE LINE

SWISS COTTAGE 49.530
ST JOHN'S WOOD 48.610

BAKER STREET
Km transfer point Jubilee to Bakerloo
46.540
BM
40B : Bakerloo Line to Queens Park

(Metropolitan, Hammersmith & City & Circle Lines cross above)

40B : Bakerloo Line to Elephant & Castle
BOND STREET 44.810
(Central Line crosses above)

(Bakerloo & Northern (CX) Lines cross above)
CHARING CROSS 42.370
41.860
NIRU / NIRJ
EB W/LOQ / WB W/LOQ
(WES) WESTMINSTER 42.020
River
Thames
Platform 3 is above 4 (District and Circle Lines cross above)

(GRP) GREEN PARK 43.350
(Victoria and Piccadilly Lines cross above)
43.320 Green Park Jn (Directions change)

Bakerloo Line controlled from Baker Street SCC

42D

D JUBILEE LINE

Stations Westminster to North Greenwich have platform edge doors

(LDB) LONDON BRIDGE 39.370
Lies below Network Rail viaducts
Twin tubes
(Northern Line (City) crosses above)

(BER) BERMONDSEY 37.440

(CAW) CANADA WATER 36.380
(East London Line crosses above)

(CKW) CANARY WHARF 33.970
(Docklands Light Railway crosses above)

(NOG) NORTH GREENWICH 32.260
River Thames

Jubilee Line controlled by TBTC from Neasden SCC

42C

(LDB) LONDON BRIDGE 39.370
(SOU) SOUTHWARK 40.620
Lies below Network Rail viaducts
(Northern Line (City) crosses above)

River Thames
(WAT) WATERLOO 41.060
(Bakerloo, Northern (CX) and Waterloo & City Lines cross above)

Jubilee Line controlled by TBTC from Neasden SCC

STRATFORD MARKET DEPOT
(Alstom Train Services Ltd)

Depot Roads:
35 Underframe cleaning
#36 & 37 Cleaning & body repairs
38-42 Inspection
43-45 Lifting

#conductor rails, other roads have overhead leads

North End
RUN-ROUND
ENGRS SDG
Depot C

Workshop
Control Tower
(TY)

ENGRS HS
ENGRS REC RD
LC
CW
DEPART
DEPOT
ARRIVAL

South End

48 : DLR to Stratford Intl.
(STR) STRATFORD 27.430
STRATFORD HIGH STREET (DLR)
STRATFORD (DLR)

ABBEY ROAD (DLR)
28.560 Staff Halt
(Dist) 30.190
44C : to Barking
NR (LTS) District Line
FSS 1
(Jub) WEST HAM (WEH) 28.970
WEST HAM (DLR/NR)
30.310 DOWN MAIN
28.750 UP MAIN
44C : to Bromley by-Bow
RUN-ROUND
HOLDING ROAD 1
HOLDING ROAD 2
HOLDING RD 3
(TY)
Temporary Fit Out Shed

STAR LANE (DLR)
(CAT) CANNING TOWN 30.550
(DLR Platforms 3 & 4 over Jubilee Line platforms - not shown)
48 : DLR to Poplar
48 : DLR

E METROPOLITAN & PICCADILLY LINES

Piccadilly Line from Rayners Lane controlled by South Kensington SCC

All distances are in kilometres unless otherwise stated in miles and chains

45C
ALPERTON 57.930
SUDBURY TOWN 59.500
SUDBURY HILL 61.150
(NR S. Harrow Tunnel under)
SOUTH HARROW 62.570 / 62.600
12m 22ch 61.900 Marylebone
South Harrow Sidings
Roxeth Viaduct
WV
43B : to Harrow-on-the-Hill
Rayners Lane Jn 64.330 (km transfer point Piccadilly to Metropolitan)
(16m 30ch #) RAYNERS LANE 64.410 (MP, MU, MW)
MP
63.500
PICCADILLY LINE

Rayners Lane Jn 64.330

EASTCOTE 66.140
RUISLIP MANOR 67.280
RUISLIP 68.000
40C : to W. Ruislip
LU Central 3 : 19A : NR
68.080
1.510
to Ruislip Depot : 40C : to S. Ruislip
RUISLIP SDG 69.480
64.100
ICKENHAM 69.850
HILLINGDON (Swakeleys) 70.930
69.110

District Railway mileage from Mansion House (via South Harrow)

Shared line controlled by Rayners Lane SC

Uxbridge Sidings
* 6m 71ch Harrow Jn (Met)
METROPOLITAN & PICCADILLY LINES
72.300 Uxbridge East Jn
73.030 UXBRIDGE *
EB / WB

43C

© Copyright **TRACKmaps**. No reproduction without permission

August 2019

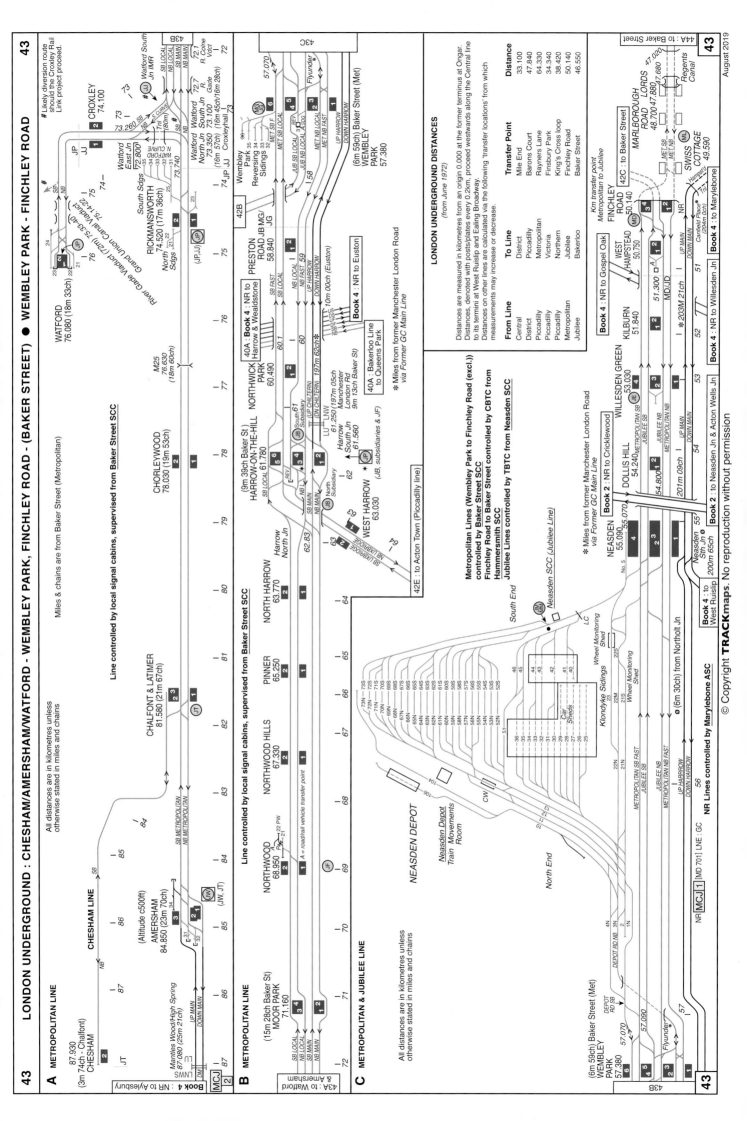

A   METROPOLITAN LINE

All distances are in kilometres unless otherwise stated in miles and chains

Miles & chains are from Baker Street (Metropolitan)

Line controlled by local signal cabins, supervised from Baker Street SCC

\# Likely diversion route should be the Croxley Rail Link project proceed.

B   METROPOLITAN LINE

Line controlled by local signal cabins, supervised from Baker Street SCC

C   METROPOLITAN & JUBILEE LINE

Line controlled by local signal cabins, supervised from Baker Street SCC

All distances are in kilometres unless otherwise stated in miles and chains

LONDON UNDERGROUND DISTANCES
(from June 1972)

Distances are measured in kilometres from an origin 0.000 at the former terminus at Ongar.
Distances, denoted with posts/plates every 0.2km, proceed westwards along the Central line to its termini at West Ruislip and Ealing Broadway.
Distances on other lines are calculated via the following 'transfer locations' from which measurements may increase or decrease.

From Line	To Line	Transfer Point	Distance
Central	District	Mile End	33.100
District	Piccadilly	Barons Court	47.840
Piccadilly	Metropolitan	Rayners Lane	64.330
Piccadilly	Victoria	Finsbury Park	34.340
Piccadilly	Northern	King's Cross loop	38.420
Metropolitan	Jubilee	Finchley Road	50.140
Jubilee	Bakerloo	Baker Street	46.550

Metropolitan Lines (Wembley Park to Finchley Road (excl.)) controlled by Baker Street SCC
Finchley Road to Baker Street controlled by CBTC from Hammersmith SCC
Jubilee Lines controlled by TBTC from Neasden SCC

* Miles from former Manchester London Road via *Former GC Main Line*

August 2019

A ALL SUB-SURFACE AND PICCADILLY LINES IN CENTRAL LONDON

All distances are in kilometres unless otherwise stated in miles and chains

Ø Common Kp point
Kp reverse to Aldgate East Jn
Kp forward to: Cromwell Curve E. Jn
Hammersmith (H & C)
Watford, Amersham, Uxbridge

$ Kilometrage meet
45.270 | 51.200
Dist. | Circle

✱ Change of Kilometrage
51.560 OR/WB | 51.620 IR/EB
45.690 | 45.590
High St Ken - Glouc Rd = 0.9km

♦ Kp reverse Earl's Court to
High St Kensington
Pfms 3 & 4
Control Centre (WV,WY-EJ,
WD-PM)

¥ = 51.700 (9m 53ch W'loo)
Acton Lane Jn

§ = This km post is
actually on the other side

¶ = Bollo Lane (Kew Line) (CCTV) 2m 63ch
Bollo Lane (Richmond Line) (MCB) 2m 63ch

49.990

Subway Tunnel

49.500

(Bakerloo Line crosses below)

48.380

Book 3 : NR over to Paddington

P / 2 1 EB WB

16 15

Book 3

14

LADBROKE GROVE 50.790

WESTBOURNE PARK

ROYAL OAK 49.000 (0m 47ch) 49

PADDINGTON

−51

50

Signal Gantry No. 3 at 0m 45ch

MLN 1 Book 3

(Elizabeth Line crosses below) 48.260

48 −49 Pra. St. 47.7

51.100

LATIMER ROAD 51.440 1 2

21L : NR to Mitre Bridge Jn

51.800

4m 48ch (Falcon Jn)

WEST LONDON LINE

WLL NR

BAYSWATER 49.240

1

(ORI) EB (R) WB

WOOD LANE 52.000 52.200

1 2

−52 (Central Line crosses below)

CIRCLE & DISTRICT LINES

NOTTING HILL GATE 50.030

50

(Central Line crosses below)

Campden Hill Tunnel

Baker Street / Earls Court

SHEPHERD'S BUSH MARKET 52.450 2

GOLDHAWK ROAD 52.970 1 2 −53

Viaduct

53.270

HAMMERSMITH DEPOT

HAMMERSMITH & CITY LINE GW & Met

53.570

Hammersmith Service Control Centre

CW

WEST LONDON EXTENSION LINE

(Kensington Jn, for Richmond ● Falcon Jn 3m 66ch (6m 63ch W'loo)

KENSINGTON OLYMPIA 47.810 3m 42ch (Falcon Jn) KENSINGTON (OLYMPIA)

DISTRICT LINE

Earl's Court Jn 47.200

44.970

HIGH STREET KENSINGTON 50.970

51.100 $

Covered Way No. 12 45.340 45.570

CIRCLE LINE 51.55

HAMMERSMITH (3m 66ch from Praed St. Jn) 53.840

Hammersmith IMR WD

EBL DIST

W. Ken West IMR WC

WEST KENSINGTON 47.180

47.120 DOWN

W. Ken East WB

2m 67·70ch

Triangle Sidings

45.790

Warwick Rd Jn 45.930

Gloucester Rd Jn 45.440

GLOUCES R

HAMMERSMITH 48.510

3 4 EBF PICC 47.410 WBF PICC

DISTRICT 48.580 PICCADILLY 49.090

44D

EB WB 47

1 EB WB

2m 62ch W. Ken East Jn 46.800

Exh. C. Pk Tnl 2m 52ch

Cromwell Road Jn

EARL'S COURT 46.270 ♦

46

(former Studland Rd Jn) 49.200

PICCADILLY 48.570 DISTRICT

Hammersmith Tunnel Former S : LSW

BARONS CT.LAY BY SDG

3 4 WBL DIST

47.840 BARONS COURT km transfer pt District to Piccadilly

old BR boundary (5m 28ch) Putney Bridge & Fulham Jn

Battery Loco Shed

2m 43ch WLL 46.710

2m 21ch

WEST BROMPTON 46.860

−47

47.260

22 : NR to Acton Wells Jn

BOK 5

SOUTH ACTON (E) 2m 48ch (Will. Jn HL)

2 1

(W) 2m 52ch S. Acton Jn

SAR 1

S : LSW

CHISWICK PARK 51.720 52§

STAMFORD BROOK 50.180

(8m 48ch W'loo)

EB LOCAL EB FAST WB FAST WB LOCAL

EB RICHMOND

45C : to Acton Town

¶

RAVENSCOURT PARK 49.440

49

50.30

Viaduct

50

LILLIE BRIDGE DEPOT Transplant

PUTNEY BRIDGE 49.430

Fulham Bridge (River Thames) 49.800

Workshop Vdct (11-19)

EB WB

WF West

24 23

31

25 27

PARSONS GREEN 48.490

(5m 13ch W'loo via E.P. reverse) (7m 00ch MH)

Parsons Green Sdgs

DISTRICT LINE

47.430

FULHAM BROADWAY 47.700 47.870

22 : NR to Clapham Jn

WEST LON WLL

−48

48.220

48.030

WF East

Earl's Court CC controls the District Lines from Ealing Broadway & Putney Bridge to High St. Ken. & Tower Hill

MH = distance from Mansion House

22 : NR to Old Kew Jn

BOK 5 (BL) (GB)

3m 12ch Gunnersbury Jn 9m 76ch (52.100)

UP KEW DOWN KEW

WB RICH.

✱ ANG LU (GB) Earl's Ct

✱ ATG

50.830 Turnham Green Jn

50.710 (8m 77ch W'loo) TURNHAM GREEN

Stores Vdct (20-32)

arches 33-44

50.400

50

−51

GUNNERSBURY 52.330 (10m 05ch)

7

22 : NR to Old Kew Jn

22 : to Clap. Jn

Kew Br. R. Thames

Miles from Waterloo via Kensington Jn to Richmond

To Putney

(7m 60ch MH) (WG) (W)

EAST PUTNEY 50.580 Pfms 1,2 6 3 4

(7m 71ch MH) East Putney Jn

(6m 03ch) 51.040

(6m 17ch) 51.320

East Putney Tunnel 284.4m (311yds)

WX

5m 55ch

PPW SW 225

21R : to Waterloo

S : LSW (W) (WG)

PBE

49.980 (7m 31ch MH)

49.580

C DISTRICT LINE

All distances are in kilometres unless otherwise stated in miles and chains

Barking Sidings (District and H&C Lines stabling) 23 22 21 20

21 22 23 24 25 26W 26E 27W 27E 28W 28E 29W 29E

Barking Sdgs West IMR FF

Barking Sdgs East IMR FF

UPNEY 23.080 2

BECONTREE 21.210 2

DAGENHAM HEATH 19.84

EB WB

Barking E. Jn

REC 30

UP CONNECTING LINE 8m 10ch Upney Jn

8m 20ch NR 1

9m 48ch

10m 3

DN CONN

DOWN CONNECTING LINE BTE

Network Rail FSS lines controlled

KEW GARDENS 54.050 (11m 10ch) 1 2

[EA 1310]

SAR 2

S : LSW

NR/DISTRICT LINE

SB (GB) 12m 20ch

22 NR

RICHMOND 56.160 (12m 39ch)

7 6 5 4 3 2 1

UP BAY

22

9m 57ch

Platforms 1,2 8 3,4,5 6 6,7 7

Controlled by NR to Gunnersbury Jn by Richmond (GB)

SOUTHFIELDS 52.130 2 1

6m 57ch

NR/DISTRICT LINE

[SW 225]

PPW S : LSW −53

WIMBLEDON PARK 53.590 2 1

7m 50ch

NR Depot

UP SIDING 2

−54

Controlled by NR to East Putney by Wimbledon ASC (W)

Wimbledon North Jn 8m 26ch

Miles from Waterloo via Wandsworth Town

LU WX

WIMBLEDON 55.150 (bs) 8m 47ch 1 2 3 4

−55

Full details of this area on 24A

C DISTRICT LINE

D PICCADILLY LINE

Controlled by Earl's Court CC

All distances are in kilometres unless otherwise stated in miles and chains

to Hammersmith

44A : to Hammersmith

EB DISTRICT 3 4 47.410 EB PICCADILLY WB PICCADILLY

1 2 WB DISTRICT

GLOUCESTER ROAD 45.420

Pfm 4 above 3

BROMPTON ROAD 44.200

5 6

4 5

4

3

43.4

47.840 BARONS COURT

46.220 EARL'S COURT

44.720 SOUTH KENSINGTON

KNIGHTSBRID

From Barons Court tunnel mouth to South Kensington the Piccadilly Line lies below the District Line

48 47 46 45 44

43C : to Finchley Road

MCL | Book 4 : NR London, St. Pancras
International & Midland City Line
Kentish Town

NR lines MCL controlled by West Hampstead (WH)

.440
WARE
ROAD
21

GREAT
PORTLAND
STREET
45.790

EUSTON
SQUARE
45.170

King's Cross
IMR
OJ

(former KING'S CROSS THAMESLINK)
1m 55ch (Moorgate)

ø These km posts are actually on the other side

46.750

MB

Baker
Street
Jn

KING'S CROSS
ST. PANCRAS
44.320

OUTER RAIL
INNER RAIL

No. 3
Clerkenwell
Tunnels
No. 2

42 ø

MOORGATE
41.330
(Northern
City Line
crosses
below)

LIVERPOOL
STREET
40.810
(Central Line
crosses
below)

40 ø

1B : East London Line

46.590

46.720
BAKER
STREET
ø
47

(Northern(CX) &
Victoria Lines
cross below)

(Piccadilly Line
crosses below)

No. 1
NR

BARBICAN
41.960

OH

0m 35ch

23

41.290

OD

Aldgate Jn
40.320

OB

ALDGATE
NORTH
CURVE

Baker St

ALDGATE
EAST
36.000

WHITECHAPEL
35.170

EN

35

34.990

(Jubilee Line
crosses below)

(Bakerloo Line
crosses below)

Ray St Gridiron
(0m 77ch)

Future
Stabling

OE

former
0m 00ch MCL

ST. MARY'S
35.500

CIRCLE, METROPOLITAN AND
HAMMERSMITH & CITY LINES

FARRINGDON
42.470 (0m 62ch) §

Smithfield
Tnl

ALDGATE
40.190

OB'EN

(St. Mary's Jn)
35.450

44B

Hammersmith to Paddington (Circle) and Euston Square/Baker Street
/Finchley Road controlled by CBTC from Hammersmith SCC
ings Cross to Aldgate/Aldgate East and Paddington (Circle) (excl.) to
tting Hill Gate controlled by Baker Street SCC

1A : NR to Blackfriars

FTL

Barbican
Tnl

Farringdon - Liverpool Street:
Elizabeth Line runs generally
under the Circle Line

OB

40.070 36.420

Minories Jn
36.430

ALDGATE
SOUTH CURVE
(Whitechapel Jn) 34.990

36

= Aldgate E. Jn
39.960] 36.080

EN

1B :
East London Line

Baker St
Earls Ct

OB

SOUTH
KENSINGTON
44.630

SLOANE SQUARE
43.390

ST. JAMES'S PARK
41.630

EMBANKMENT
40.180

39.480
TEMPLE

CANNON ST.
37.810

EG

MARK
LANE

EJ (m)

TOWER HILL
36.800

(IR)

EF

Street
level

EH

★ former ALDGATE EAST 36.200 District Line

44.880
44.330

43.180-220

42.350
VICTORIA
(Victoria Line
crosses below)

40.870
WESTMINSTER
(Jubilee Line
crosses below)

(Bakerloo &
Northern,
CX Branch
cross below
& NR above)

38.720
BLACKFRIARS
(NR crosses
above, W&C
below)

38.120
MANSION
HOUSE

37.470
MONUMENT
(Northern Line,
City Branch
crosses below)

S Distance back from Rayners Lane
Aldgate East - Liverpool St.: 0·93km
Aldgate - Tower Hill 0·50km

est Ken - Sth Ken:
e Piccadilly Line runs
low the District Line

CIRCLE &
DISTRICT LINES

45   44   43   42   41   40   39   38   37

34   33   GFB   32   31   30   29   28   27   26   25   24

Book 2 : NR to Stratford

41B : Central Line

48 : DLR
to Stratford

BROMLEY
BY-BOW
31.580

39D : to
Stratford

48 : DLR to
Stratford Intl.

Controlled from Barking SC (FB - FF)

Book 2 : NR to Woodgrange Park

Signals
LU only

DISTRICT LINE

13m 62ch (St Pancras)

TEPNEY
GREEN
34.170

BOW
CH

FB

WEST HAM
30.190 EB

PLAISTOW
29.390 FC

UPTON PARK
28.150

EAST HAM
26.740 FE

River
Roding

13m 12ch

13m 12ch
(Barking
Stn Jn)

TAH 4

13m 18ch

FF (FB-FG)

BAY PLAT. LINE
ANG LU

1

RECEPTION
30

32.000   31.200   30.350

DOWN MAIN
UP MAIN

NR

East Ham
Depot

25.400

DOWN MAIN
UP MAIN

33.130
MILE END
Gas Factory Jn

32.590
BOW RD

2m 77ch   3m 37ch   4m 01ch

R. Lea
& Bow
Creek

4m 07ch

WB
DN TILBURY

35

Book 2 : NR to Fenchurch St

★ km transfer point
Central to District

2m
57ch
3m 18ch

48 : DLR to
Poplar

4m 45ch   5m 28ch

FSS 1

LMS : Mid (LTS)
Miles from Fenchurch Street

6m 22ch

BWT

7m
06ch

Barking
W Jn
7m 08ch

7m 33ch
Barking
Tilbury Line
Jn West

13m 42ch

UP   TILBURY

24.550   7m 60ch

7m 42ch
BARKING

7m 65ch
Barking
Tilbury Line
Jn East

distances are in kilometres unless
erwise stated in miles and chains

39D : Jubilee
Line to Waterloo
& Stanmore

48 : DLR to
Canning Town etc.

Network Rail FSS and part GFB lines controlled by Upminster SC (UR)

1 FSS 2

Book 2 : NR to Grays

DISTRICT AND HAMMERSMITH & CITY LINES

TLL

UPMINSTER
DEPOT

WME: Wheel Monitoring
Equipment Shed

Car Shed

Lifting Shed

11.180

11.320

11.080

District Line controlled from Barking SC (FF - FG) and Upminster SC (FJ, FM)

Controlled by
Liverpool Street IECC (L)

18   17   16   15   14   13   3m 30ch
(Romford)   12

Depot Control
Tower

11.120

Book 2 :
NR to Romford

ROU

UPMINSTER
12.190

FM (FJ-FM)

FM DCT

WME

DAGENHAM
EAST
18.500 FG

ELM PARK
16.170

HORNCHURCH
14.660 FJ

UPMINSTER
BRIDGE
13.410

West IMR

FM   4   5

ICW

Cleaning Shed

Wheel Lathe

DG 5

12m 57ch   14m 38ch

DOWN MAIN
UP MAIN

Upminster East Jn

DOWN MAIN
UP MAIN

NR

11m 60ch
Dagenham East
Crossovers

11m 25ch

13m 56ch

15m 39ch

0m 00ch

15m 20ch

1A

U. SDG

OCKENDON
UP DN

15m 38ch

FSS 2

LMS : Mid (LTS)
Miles from Fenchurch Street

IECC (UR)

UPG

FSS 2   LMS : Mid (LTS)

ster SC (UR)

Book 2 : NR to Grays

46B : Northern (City) Line to Euston

KING'S
CROSS
LOOP

38.42km transfer pt
via Kings Cross Loop
Piccadilly to Northern

L

King's Cross IMR (m)

CALEDONIAN
ROAD
36.380

(ex GILLESPIE ROAD)

ARSENAL
35.040

VIC NB
VIC SB
PIC EB

VK

34.550

33.180

YDE
ARK
.970

GREEN PARK
41.910
(Jubilee Line
crosses below
and Victoria
Line above)

LEICESTER
SQUARE
40.840
(Central Line
crosses above)

39.890

HOLBORN
40.010

RUSSELL
SQUARE
39.260

38.590

KING'S
CROSS
ST. PANCRAS
38.340

YORK
ROAD
37.700

Twin tubes

HOLLOWAY
ROAD
35.780

FINSBURY
PARK
34.340

MANOR
HOUSE
33.300

45D

PB (e)

PD

(Northern,
CX crosses above)

(closed 1 Oct 1994)

(Circle/H. & C./Met
and Victoria Lines
cross above, the
Northern (City) Line below)

From King's Cross to Finsbury Park
the Piccadilly Line lies below the
East Coast Main Line

47C : Victoria Line
to Brixton

47C : Victoria Line
to Walthamstow

42.480
DOWN STREET

41.370
PICCADILLY
CIRCUS
(Bakerloo Line
crosses above)

40.580
COVENT
GARDEN

40.840
ALDWYCH (STRAND)

ø Holborn, King's Cross, Finsbury Park - although line directions
are Eastbound and Westbound, passenger information refers
to 'Northbound' and 'Southbound' respectively

Km transfer point
Piccadilly to Victoria

43   42   41   40   39   38   37   36   35   34   33

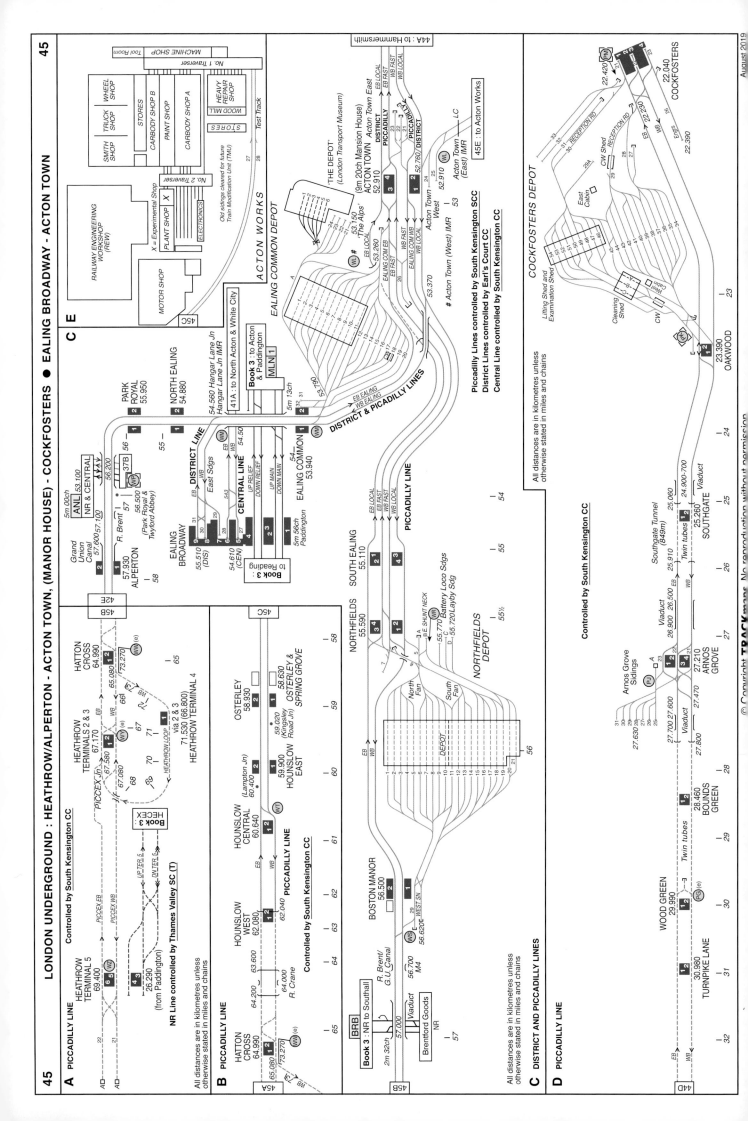

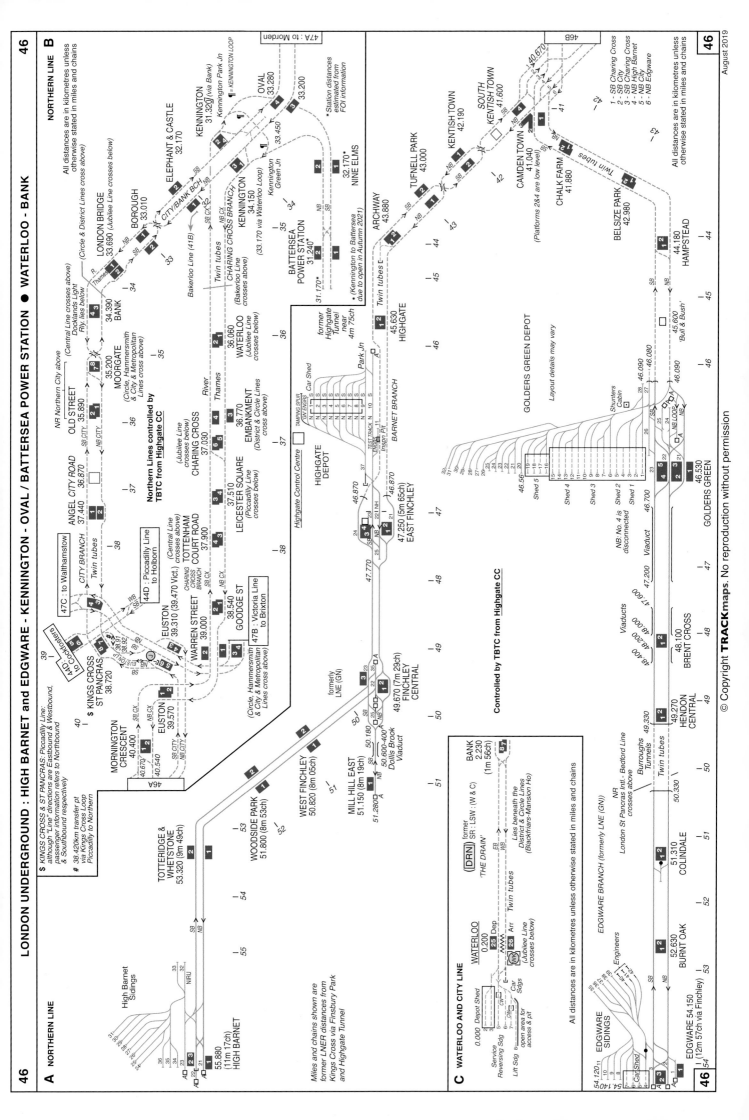

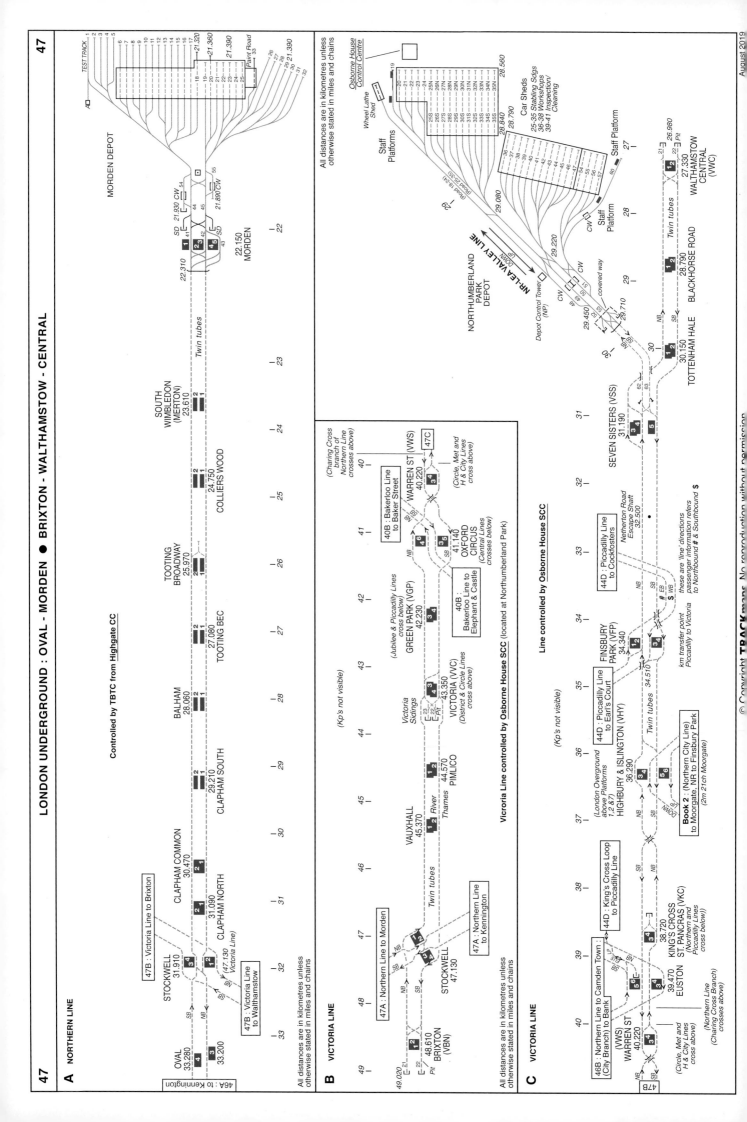

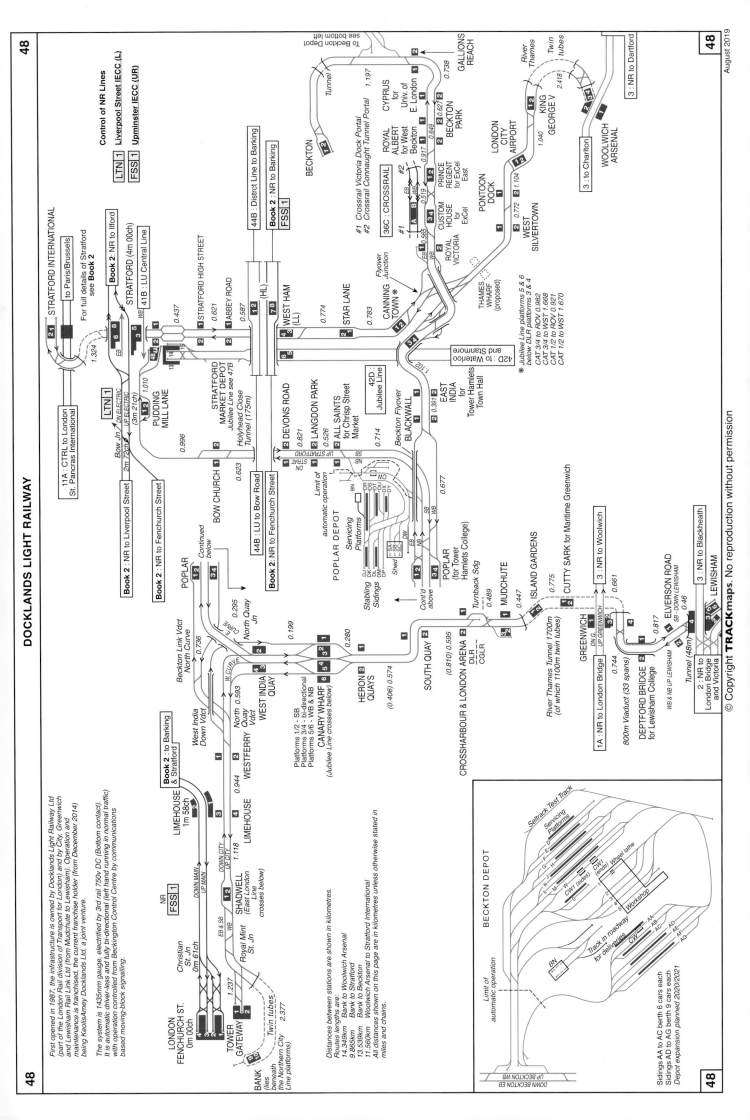

First opened in 1987, the infrastructure is owned by Docklands Light Railway Ltd (part of the London Rail division of Transport for London) and by City, Greenwich and Lewisham Rail Link Ltd (from Mudchute to Lewisham). Operation and maintenance is franchised, the current franchise holder (from December 2014) being KeolisAmey Docklands Ltd, a joint venture.

The system is 1435mm gauge, electrified by 3rd rail 750v DC (Bottom contact). It is automatic driver-less and fully bi-directional (left hand running in normal traffic) with operation controlled from Beckington Control Centre by communications based moving-block signalling.

Control of NR Lines
Liverpool Street IECC (L)
Upminster IECC (UR)

LTN 1   FSS 1

STRATFORD INTERNATIONAL
to Paris/Brussels

11A : CTRL to London
St. Pancras International

For full details of Stratford see **Book 2**

STRATFORD (4m 00ch)

Book 2 : NR to Ilford
41B : LU Central Line
44B : District Line to Barking
Book 2 : NR to Barking

STRATFORD HIGH STREET
ABBEY ROAD
WEST HAM (LL)
(HL)
STAR LANE
CANNING TOWN *
Flyover Junction

THAMES WHARF (proposed)

PUDDING MILL LANE
LTN 1
UP ELECTRIC
DN ELECTRIC
(3m 21ch)
Bow Jn
2m 72ch

STRATFORD MARKET DEPOT
Jubilee Line see 47B
Holyhead Close Tunnel (175m)

Book 2 : NR to Liverpool Street
Book 2 : NR to Fenchurch Street

BOW CHURCH
DEVONS ROAD
LANGDON PARK
ALL SAINTS for Chrisp Street Market
44B : LU to Bow Road
UP STRATFORD
DN STRAT

BLACKWALL
Beckton Flyover
EAST INDIA for Tower Hamlets Town Hall
42D : Jubilee Line
42D : to Jubilee Line

POPLAR
Continued below
North Quay Jn
Beckton Link Vdct North Curve
E. CURVE
W. CURVE

POPLAR DEPOT
Servicing Platforms
Stabling Sidings
Limit of automatic operation

POPLAR (for Tower Hamlets College)
Cont'd above
Turnback Sdg

MUDCHUTE
ISLAND GARDENS
CUTTY SARK for Maritime Greenwich
GREENWICH
River Thames Tunnel 1700m (of which 1100m twin tubes)

3 : NR to Woolwich
1A : NR to London Bridge
DEPTFORD BRIDGE for Lewisham College
800m Viaduct (33 spans)

ELVERSON ROAD
SB- DOWN LEWISHAM
Tunnel (48m)
LEWISHAM
3 : NR to Blackheath
2 : NR to London Bridge and Victoria

SOUTH QUAY
CROSSHARBOUR & LONDON ARENA
DLR CGLR
HERON QUAYS

Platforms 1/2 - SB
Platforms 3/4 - bi-directional
Platforms 5/6 - WB & NB
(Jubilee Line crosses below)

CANARY WHARF
WEST INDIA QUAY
North Quay Vdct
West India Down Vdct
WESTFERRY
LIMEHOUSE
North Jn

LIMEHOUSE
1m 58ch
SHADWELL (East London Line crosses below)
NR
FSS 1
DOWN MAIN
UP MAIN
DOWN CITY
UP CITY
EB & SB
WB

Christian St. Jn
0m 61ch
Royal Mint St. Jn

Book 2 : to Barking & Stratford

LONDON FENCHURCH ST.
0m 00ch
TOWER GATEWAY
BANK (lies beneath the Northern City Line platforms)
Twin tubes

Distances between stations are shown in kilometres.

Routes lengths are:
14.349km   Bank to Woolwich Arsenal
9.865km   Bank to Stratford
13.539km   Bank to Beckton
11.560km   Woolwich Arsenal to Stratford International
All distances shown on this page are in kilometres unless otherwise stated in miles and chains.

To Beckton Depot see bottom left

GALLIONS REACH
BECKTON
Tunnel
BECKTON PARK
CYPRUS for Univ. of E. London
ROYAL ALBERT for West Beckton
CUSTOM HOUSE for ExCeL
PRINCE REGENT for ExCeL East
ROYAL VICTORIA
ROYAL ALBERT

ROYAL VICTORIA Dock Portal
Crossrail Connaught Tunnel Portal

#1 Crossrail Victoria Dock Portal
#2 Crossrail Connaught Tunnel Portal

36C : CROSSRAIL
#1   #2

River Thames
Twin tubes
KING GEORGE V
3 : NR to Dartford
3 : to Charlton
WOOLWICH ARSENAL

LONDON CITY AIRPORT
PONTOON DOCK
WEST SILVERTOWN

42D : to Waterloo and Stanmore

* Jubilee Line platforms 5 & 6 below DLR platforms 3 & 4
CAT 3/4 to ROV 0.982
CAT 3/4 to WST 1.668
CAT 1/2 to ROV 0.921
CAT 1/2 to WST 1.670

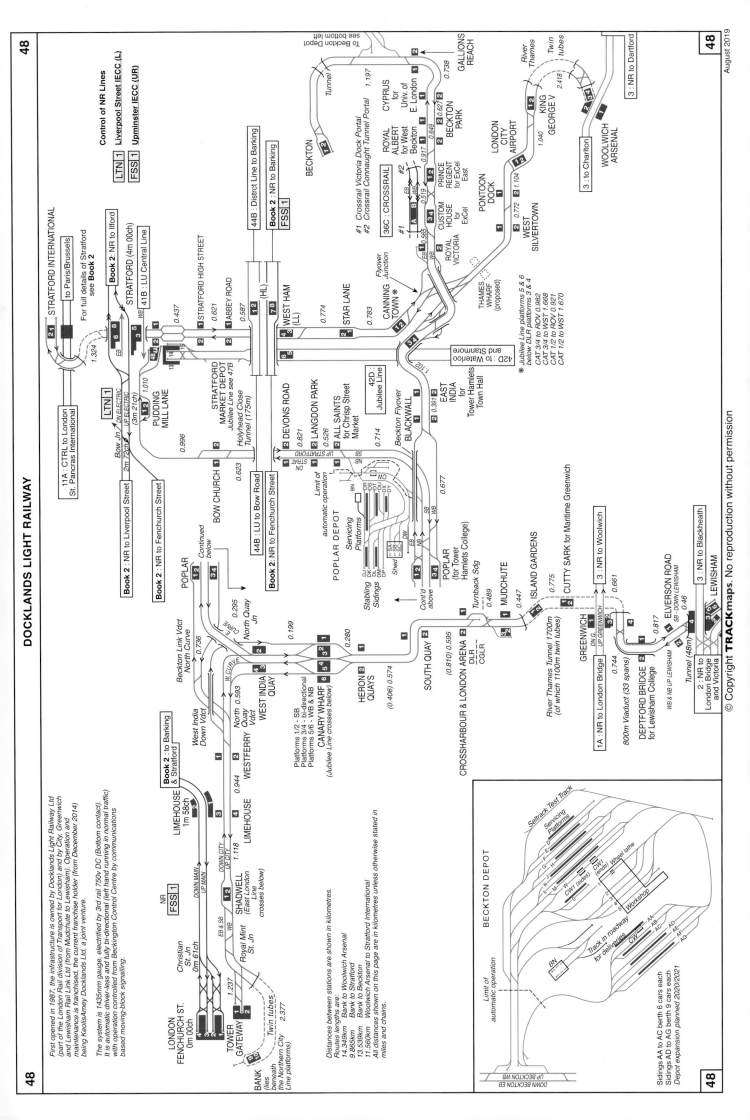

BECKTON DEPOT
Seltrack Test Track
Servicing Platforms
Workshop
CW1 (sides)
CW1 (ends)
Wheel lathe
Track in roadway for deliveries
Limit of automatic operation
BN
DOWN BECKTON EB
UP BECKTON WB

Sidings AA to AC berth 6 cars each
Sidings AD to AG berth 9 cars each
Depot expansion planned 2020/2021

© Copyright **TRACKmaps**. No reproduction without permission

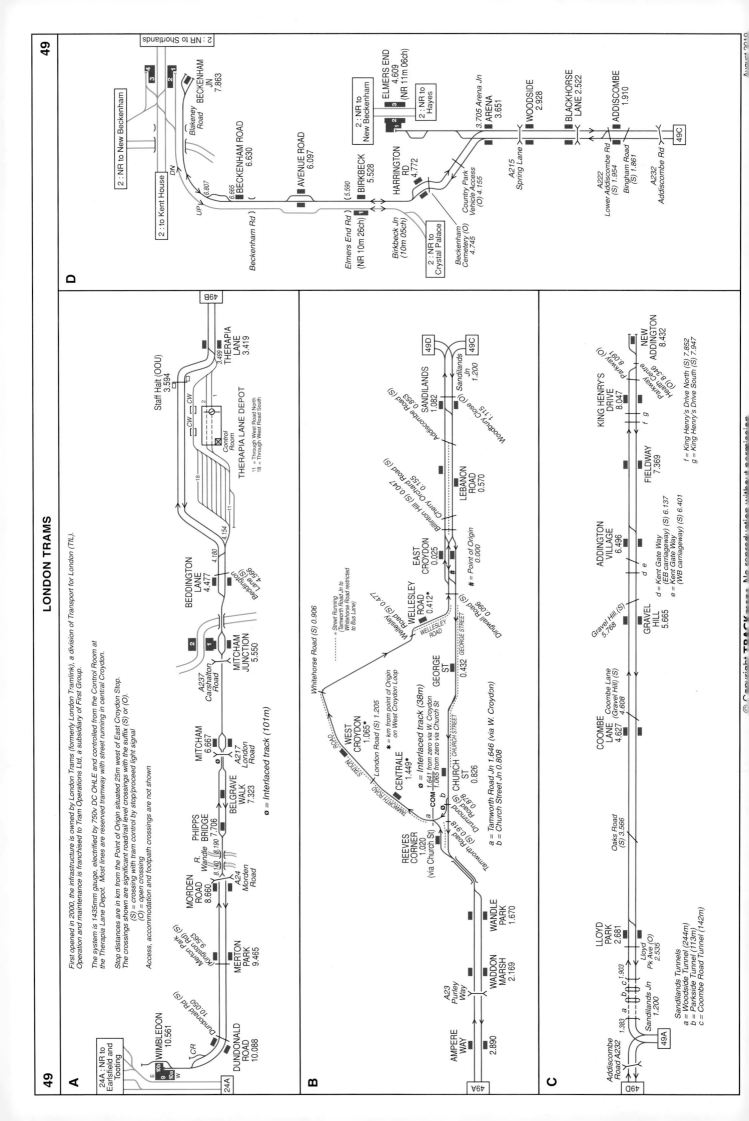

A

First opened in 2000, the infrastructure is owned by London Trams (formerly London Tramlink), a division of Transport for London (TfL).
Operation and maintenance is franchised to Tram Operations Ltd, a subsidiary of First Group.

The system is 1435mm gauge, electrified by 750v DC OHLE and controlled from the Control Room at the Therapia Lane Depot. Most lines are reserved tramway with street running in central Croydon.

Stop distances are in km from the Point of Origin situated 25cm west of East Croydon Stop.
The crossings shown are significant road/rail level crossings with the suffix (S) or (O).
  (S) = crossing with tram control by stop/proceed light signal
  (O) = open crossing
Access, accommodation and footpath crossings are not shown.

24A : NR to Earlsfield and Tooting

WIMBLEDON 10.561
Dundonald Rd (S) 10.250
DUNDONALD ROAD 10.088
Merton Park (S) 9.563
Kingston Rd (S) 9.563
MERTON PARK 9.465
MORDEN ROAD 8.660
A24 Morden Road
R. Wandle 8.140
PHIPPS BRIDGE 8.190 7.706
BELGRAVE WALK 7.323
MITCHAM 6.667
A217 London Road
A237 Carshalton Road
MITCHAM JUNCTION 5.550
BEDDINGTON LANE 4.477
Beddington Lane (S) 4.566
THERAPIA LANE 3.419
3.499
3.594 Staff Halt (OOU)
THERAPIA LANE DEPOT
Control Room
CW CW
11 = Through West Road North
18 = Through West Road South
4.180
4.154
ø = Interlaced track (101m)

B

49B

Whitehorse Road (S) 0.906
WEST CROYDON 1.065*
London Road (S) 1.205
CENTRALE 1.449*
ø = Interlaced track (38m)
* = km from zero via W. Croydon on West Croydon Loop
REEVES CORNER 1.020 (via Church St)
Tamworth Road
Station Road
Drummond Road 0.918
CHURCH ST 0.826
a—COM 1.641 from zero via W. Croydon
1.065 from zero via Church St
b 0.819
GEORGE ST
CHURCH STREET
GEORGE STREET 0.432
WELLESLEY ROAD 0.412*
Wellesley Road (S) 0.477
Dingwall Road 0.096
EAST CROYDON 0.025
# = Point of Origin
0.000 = Point of Origin
Billinton Hill (S) 0.047
Cherry Orchard Road (S) 0.155
LEBANON ROAD 0.570
= Street Running (Tamworth Road Jn to Whitehorse Road restricted to Bus Lane)
Tamworth Road Jn 1.646 (via W. Croydon)
Church Street Jn 0.808
a = Tamworth Road (S)
b = Church Street
Addiscombe Road (S) 0.853
SANDILANDS 1.082
Woodbury Close (O) 1.115
Sandilands Jn 1.200
49D
49C
49A

AMPERE WAY 2.890
A23 Purley Way
WADDON MARSH 2.169
WANDLE PARK 1.670

C

Addiscombe Road A232
Sandilands Jn 1.200
49A
Sandilands Tunnels
a = Woodside Tunnel (244m)
b = Parkside Tunnel (113m)
c = Coombe Road Tunnel (142m)
1.383 a b c 1.903
Lloyd Pk Ave (O) 2.535
LLOYD PARK 2.681
Oaks Road (S) 3.566
COOMBE LANE 4.627
Coombe Lane (Gravel Hill) (S) 4.608
GRAVEL HILL 5.665
Gravel Hill (S) 5.768
ADDINGTON VILLAGE 6.496
d = Kent Gate Way (EB carriageway) (S) 6.137
e = Kent Gate Way (WB carriageway) (S) 6.401
d e
FIELDWAY 7.369
KING HENRY'S DRIVE 8.047
f g
f = King Henry's Drive North (S) 7.852
g = King Henry's Drive South (S) 7.947
Parkway (O) 8.091
Parkway Centre 8.346
Fieldway Centre (O) 8.346
NEW ADDINGTON 8.432
49C

D

2 : NR to Shortlands
4 3 2 1
BECKENHAM JN 7.863
Blakeney Road
2 : to New Beckenham
2 : to Kent House
6.807
6.665
DN
UP
BECKENHAM ROAD 6.630
AVENUE ROAD 6.097
BIRKBECK 5.528
(5.590)
Beckenham Rd)
Elmers End Rd) (NR 10m 26ch)
Birkbeck Jn (10m 05ch)
2 : NR to Crystal Palace
HARRINGTON RD 4.772
ELMERS END 4.609 (NR 11m 06ch)
2 : NR to Hayes
3 1 2
2 : NR to New Beckenham
3.705 Arena Jn
ARENA 3.651
Country Park Vehicle Access (O) 4.155
Beckenham Cemetery (O) 4.745
WOODSIDE 2.928
A215 Spring Lane
BLACKHORSE LANE 2.522
A222 Lower Addiscombe Rd (S) 1.954
ADDISCOMBE 1.910
Bingham Road (S) 1.861
A232 Addiscombe Rd
49C

August 2018

© Copyright TRACKmaps. No reproduction without permission

Index

This index covers practically all the named locations relating to the National Network which appear on the maps to assist the reader in their search. Stations are listed in capitals, signal boxes with their codes and level crossings with their type. Some BW and FP crossings in the maps have been carried to the index together with some road and motorway bridges, but not all. The approaches to the London Termini include over 130 viaducts and arches which are named on the maps but excluded from this Index. Locations of now-defunct assets are given in brackets. Other public service lines, light rail, heritage lines, narrow gauge and other private lines are indexed by their line name and key stations only.

Location	Code
London Road Viaduct (Brighton)	16A
London Road Viaduct (Guildford)	26
LONDON ST.PANCRAS INTERNATIONAL	11A
LONDON TRANSPORT MUSEUM ('THE DEPOT')	45C
London Tunnel 1 (CTRL)	11B
London Tunnel 2 (CTRL)	11C
LONDON VICTORIA	21A
LONDON WATERLOO	21A
Long Salts LC (UWC)	7A
Long Valley Sdg	30B
LONGCROSS	28A
LONGFIELD	5
Longford River Bridge (Feltham)	28A
Longford River Bridge (Hampton)	24B
Longhedge Jns	21A
Loover Barn No.2 LC (UWC)	17A
LORDS (LU-Met) (disused)	43C
Loughborough Jn	2
LOUGHBOROUGH JUNCTION	2
LOUGHTON (LU-Cent)	41C
Lovers Walk SB (L)	16A
Lower Barn No.1 LC (UWC)	17A
Lower Shakespeare Cliff Shaft (Eurotunnel)	13B
LOWER SYDENHAM	2
Lucas Street Tunnel (North portal)	1A
Lucas Street Tunnel (South portal)	2
Ludgate GW Jn	21A
Ludgate Line Viaduct	21A
LUDGERSHALL (disused)	35A
Ludgershall DSDA MOD (Army)	35A
(Lullingstone)	4A
Lupin Intersection Bridge	14C
Luton Arch	6A
LYDD TOWN (disused)	18D
Lydd Town LC (TMOG)	18D
Lydden Tunnel	10
(Lymington Jn)	33B
LYMINGTON PIER	33B
Lymington Pier LC (UWC)	33B
Lymington River Bridge (Brockenhurst)	33A
LYMINGTON TOWN	33B
Lymington Town LC (CCTV)	33B
Lymington Viaduct	33B
Lyminster LC (CCTV)	23B
Lyne Bridge (M25) Bridge	28A

M

Location	Code
M2 Bridge (Cuxton)	5
M2 Bridge (Selling)	6A
M2/CTRL Bridge (Cuxton)	5
M20 Bridge (Ashford)	9B
M20 Bridge (Aylesford)	5
M20 Bridge (Charing)	9A
M20 Bridge (Westenhanger)	9B
M20/CTRL Bridge (Bearsted)	9A
M23 Bridge (Balcombe Tunnel Jn)	15B
M23 Bridge (Coopers Hill Viaduct)	8A
M25 Bridge (Ashtead)	25
M25 Bridge (Byfleet)	24B
M25 Bridge (Egham)	28A
M25 Bridge (Eynsford)	5
M25 Bridge (Lyne Bridge)	28A
M25 Bridge (Merstham)	15A
M25 Bridge (Swanley)	4A
M25 Bridge (Wraysbury)	28A
M26 Bridge (Dunton Green)	4A
M26 Bridge (Otford)	4A
M27 (Portchester)	29C
M27 Bridge (Fareham Tunnels)	29C
M27 Bridge (Romsey)	35C
M27 Bridge (Southampton Apt P'way)	32A
M3 (Blackwater)	27C
M3 (Winchfield)	27C
M3 Bridge (Chandler's Ford)	35C
M3 Bridge (Shawford)	30C
M3 Bridge (Virginia Water)	28A
M4 Bridge (Green Park)	30A
M4 Bridge (Kew East Jn)	22
M4 Bridge (Winnersh)	28B
MAIDA VALE (LU-Bak)	40B
Maiden LC (Elm Lane)(CCTV)	24B
MAIDEN NEWTON	37A
MAIDSTONE BARRACKS	5
MAIDSTONE EAST	5
Maidstone East SB (ME)	5
MAIDSTONE WEST	5
Maidstone West SB (MS)	5
MAIL RAIL (Royal Mail)	38A
Mair No.2 LC (UWC)	18C
MALDEN MANOR	25
MANNEZ QUARRY (Alderney Rly)	17C
MANOR HOUSE (LU-Pic)	44D
MANSION HOUSE (LU-Dist+Circ)	44A
Manston Jn	7A
Manston Road Bridge (Br1961A)(Ramsgate)	7A
Mantles Wood (LU-Met)	43A
MARBLE ARCH (LU-Cent)	41B
Marchwood Military Port	33A
Marchwood SB (MW)	33A
MARDEN	8C
MARGATE for Cliftonville	7A
Maritime East Jn	33A
Maritime Freightliner Terminal	33A
Maritime Way LC	32A
Maritime West Jn	33A
Mark Beech Tunnel	14B
MARLBOROUGH ROAD (LU-Met) (disused)	43C
Marley Lane LC (CCTV)	18B
Marshwood Farm No.2 LC (UWC)	36E
(Marston Magna)	37B
Martello Tunnel	10
MARTIN MILL	10
MARTINS HERON	28B
MARYLAND	39B
MARYLEBONE (LU-Bak)	40B
Mays LC (CCTV)	28A
MAZE HILL	1A
McDougall LC (UWC)(NT)	8C
McGee No.2 LC (UWC)	33A
McGee No.3 LC (UWC)	33A
McGee No.4 LC (UWC)	33A
Meads Farm LC (UWC)	37A
Medhurst Row LC (FP)(MSL-X)	8A
MEDSTEAD & FOUR MARKS (MHR)	27D
Medway River Bridge (Ashurst)	14B
Medway River Bridge (Beltring)	8C
Medway River Bridge (Maidstone)	5
Medway River Bridge (Rochester)	5
Medway River Bridge (Tonbridge)	4B
Medway River Bridges (Tonbridge)	8B
Medway Viaduct (Leigh)	8B
Melcombe Regis LC (open)	34D
Meon River Bridge (Swanwick)	29C
MEOPHAM	5
Merrick No.2 LC (UWC)	18C
Merrick No.3 LC (UWC)	18C
(Merrow)	26
Mersham Tunnel	9B
Mersham Tunnel (CTRL)	12C
MERSTHAM	15A
Merstham Tunnel	15A
MERTON PARK (LTrams)	49A
Metropolitan Jn	1A
METROPOLITAN LINE (LU-Met)	43A
MICHELDEVER	30C
Micheldever LC (FP)	30C
Mickleham Tunnel	25
Middle Jn (Sittingbourne)	6B
Middle LC (MCB) (Deal)	7A
Middle Road LC (UWC)	36A
(Middle Stoke)	5
Middle Stoke LC (UWC)	5
MID-HANTS RAILWAY (MHR)	27D
Midley LC (open)	18D
(Milborne Port)	36C
Mile Drove LC (UWC)	7A
MILE END (LU-Cent)	41B
MILE END (LU-Dist+H&C)	44B
Mile End Shaft (Crossrail)	39B
MILFORD	29A
Milford LC (AHBC)	29A
MILL HILL EAST (LU-Northn)	46A
Mill Lane Viaduct (Carshalton)	25
Mill Road Viaduct (Lewisham)	2
MILLBROOK	32A
Millbrook Freightliner Terminal	32A
Milstead LC	8C
Milton Court LC (UWC)	27B
(Milton Range)	5
Minories Jn (LU)	44A
MINSTER	7A
Minster SB (EBE)	7A
Minster South Jn	7A
Minster West Jn	7A
MITCHAM (LTrams)	49A
MITCHAM EASTFIELDS	25
MITCHAM JUNCTION	25
MITCHAM JUNCTION (LTrams)	49A
Mitre Bridge Jn	21B
Mitre Bridge LC (CCTV)	21B
Mitre Tunnel	21B
Mole River Bridge - 4 arch (Boxhill)	25
Mole River Bridge (Cobham)	25
Mole River Bridge (Hersham)	24B
Mole River Bridge (Leatherhead)	25
Mole Viaduct (Dorking)	27B
Mole Viaduct (Leatherhead)	25
MONKTON & CAME (disused)	34D
Monkton Parsonage LC (UWC)	7A
Montpelier Junction	16A
MONUMENT (LU-Dist+Circ)	44A
Monxton Viaduct	35A
MOOR PARK (LU-Met)	43B
Moores LC (UWC)	18D
MOORGATE (LU-Circ+Dist+H&C)	44A
MOORGATE (LU-Northn)	46B
MORDEN (LU-Northn)	47A
Morden Depot (LU-Northn)	47A
MORDEN ROAD	25
MORDEN ROAD (LTrams)	49A
MORDEN SOUTH	25
MORETON (Dorset)	34C
Moreton LC (AHBC-X)	34C
MORNINGTON CRESCENT (LU-Northn)	46B
Morris Farm No.2 LC (UWC)	36B
MORTIMER	30A
MORTLAKE	22
MOTSPUR PARK	25
Motspur Park Jn	25
Motspur Park LC (CCTV)	25
MOTTINGHAM	3
MOTTISFONT & DUNBRIDGE	35C
MOULSECOOMB	16A
Mount Pleasant LC (CCTV)	32A
Mount Pleasant Tunnel	18C
Mount Street Tunnel	3
Mountain LC (open)	18D
Mountbatten Way Bridge (Millbrook)	32A
Mountfield Sdgs	18B
Mountfield Sdgs GF 'MF'	18B
Mountfield Tunnel	18B
MUDCHUTE (DLR)	48
Muggeridge LC (UWC)	5

N

Location	Code
Nashenden Crossovers (CTRL)	11E
Nashenden Signal Room (CTRL)	11E
NEASDEN (LU-Met+Jub)	43C
Neasden Depot (LU-Met+Jub)	43C
Neasden SCC (LU-Jub)	43C
Neasden South Jn	43C
NETLEY	32A
Netley GF 'B'	32A
NEW ADDINGTON (LTrams)	49C
New Barn LC (UWC)	23C
NEW BECKENHAM	2
New Beckenham Jn	2
NEW CROSS	1A
NEW CROSS GATE	1A
New Cross Gate Depot	1A
New Cross Gate Down Jn	1A
New Cross Gate North Jn	1A
New Cross Gate Up Jn	1A
NEW ELTHAM	3
New Fishbourne LC (AHBC)	23D
New Harbour Road LC	34B
NEW HYTHE	5
New Kew Jn	22
NEW MALDEN	24B
NEW MILTON	34A
NEW ROMNEY (RHDR)	18E
(New Wandsworth Goods)	2
New Yard Depot (Exeter)	37D
NEWBURY PARK (LU-Cent)	41C
NEWHAVEN HARBOUR	17A
Newhaven Harbour Jn	17A
NEWHAVEN MARINE (disused)	17A
NEWHAVEN TOWN	17A
Newhaven Town LC (CCTV)	17A
NEWINGTON	6A
Newington Road Bridge (Br.1962)(Ramsgate)	7A
Newtown Berthing Sdgs	9B
NINE ELMS (LU-Northn)	46B
Nine Elms International Flyover	21A
Nine Elms Jn	21A
Nine Elms Viaduct	21A
NORBITON	24B
NORBURY	2
NORDEN (SWGR)	20D
NORMANS BAY	17B
NORTH ACTON (LU-Cent)	41A
North Acton Jn (LU-Cent)	41A
North Approach Viaduct	21A
North Bank Viaduct	1A
NORTH CAMP	27C
North Camp LC (CCTV)	27C
North Downs Tunnel (Blue Bell Hill) (CTRL)	11E
North Downs Tunnel (CTRL)	12A
NORTH DULWICH	2
North Dulwich Viaduct	2
NORTH EALING (LU-Pic)	45C
NORTH GREENWICH (LU-Jub)	42D
North Halling LC (MSL)	5
NORTH HARROW (LU-Met)	43B
North Kent East Jn	1A
North Kent Line connection (CTRL)	11D
North Pole Depot (Hitachi Rail Europe)	21B
North Pole Jn	21B
North Quay Jn (DLR)	48
North Quay Viaduct (DLR)	48
NORTH SHEEN	22
North Sheen LC (CCTV)	22
North Stoke Tunnel	19D
North Wall LC (MSL)	7A
NORTH WEALD (EOR)	40D
NORTH WEMBLEY (LU-Bak)	40A
North Woolwich Portal (Crossrail)	39C
(Northam)	32A
Northam Jn	32A
Northam Road Bridge	32A
Northam Traincare Facility	32A
NORTHERN LINE (LU-Northn)	46
NORTHFIELDS (LU-Pic)	43B
Northfields Depot (LU-Pic)	43B
NORTHFLEET	5
Northfleet Cement Works	5
Northfleet Jn	5
Northfleet Southern Bypass Bridge	5
NORTHIAM (KESR)	20C
NORTHOLT (LU-Cent)	40C
Northumberland Park Depot (LU-Vic)	47C
NORTHWICK PARK (LU-Met)	43B
NORTHWOOD (LU-Met)	43B
NORTHWOOD HILLS (LU-Met)	43B
Norway Lane LC (UWC)	23B
Norwood Cable Depot LC (UWC)	2
Norwood Fork Jns	14C
NORWOOD JUNCTION	2
Norwood North Junctions	2
NOTTING HILL GATE (LU-Dist+Circ)	44A
NOTTING HILL GATE (LU-Cent)	41A
NUNHEAD	2
Nunhead Jn	2
(Nursling)	35C
Nutbourne LC (AHBC)	23D
NUTBOURNE	23D
NUTFIELD	8A

Line of Route Codes

Lines on the Network are nowadays given a Line of Route code (LOR) which may run over a number of ELRs. LORs have their origin in the codes used in the early 1990's in BR's Western Region. These were extended nationally by Railtrack in the late 1990's as Possession Resource Information Database (PRIDE) codes and renamed LOR sometime after. More information can be found about these codes on the excellent website by Phil Deaves (see Bibliography). The LOR description is the one generally used within the industry. To find an LOR in this book, take the location name from the list below and search for it in the Location Index.

Kent/Sussex codes appearing in this book

SO110	Victoria Eastern to Ramsgate (via Herne Hill and Chatham)
SO130	Charing Cross/Cannon Street to Dover Priory/Eurotunnel interface (via Tonbridge)
SO140	Swanley to Ashford
SO150	Sittingbourne Western Jn to Sheerness-on-Sea
SO160	Faversham to Dover Priory
SO170	Tonbridge to Bo Peep Junction
SO180	Paddock Wood to Strood
SO210	Appledore to Lydd Town (Goods Line)
SO220	Ashford to Ramsgate (via Canterbury West)
SO230	Folkestone East to Folkestone Harbour
SO240	Buckland Jn to Minster East Jn
SO250	Factory Jn/Battersea Pier Jn/Clapham Junction to Wembley Central
SO260	Brixton Jn to Shortlands Jn (Catford Loop)
SO280	Farringdon to Herne Hill
SO290	North Kent East Jn to Dartford Jn(via Greenwich)
SO300	Lewisham Jn to Crayford Creek Jn (via Bexleyheath)
SO310	Hither Green to Rochester Bridge Jn (via Sidcup)
SO320	Hoo Junction to Grain (Goods Line)
SO330	Nunhead to Hayes
SO350	Grove Park to Bromley North
SO400	St Pancras to Eurotunnel Interface
SO500	Victoria to Brighton
SO510	London Bridge to Epsom Downs
SO520	Three Bridges to Portsmouth Harbour (via Horsham)
SO530	South Croydon Jn to East Grinstead
SO540	Hurst Green Junction to Uckfield
SO550	Redhill to Tonbridge
SO560	Redhill to Guildford
SO590	Keymer Jn to Eastbourne
SO600	Willingdon Jn to Ashford
SO620	Brighton to Lewes
SO630	Brighton/Preston Park to Littlehampton
SO640	Barnham to Bognor Regis
SO645	Battersea Park to Peckham Rye (Atlantic Lines)
SO650	Balham Jn to Beckenham Junction/Norwood Junction
SO660	Purley to Caterham & Chipstead Line Jn (Purley) to Tattenham Corner
SO680	South Bermondsey Jn to Horsham
SO700	Streatham South Jn to Sutton (via Wimbledon)

Wessex codes appearing in this book

SW100	Waterloo to Clapham Junction
SW105	Clapham Junction to Weymouth
SW110	Woking Junction to Portsmouth Harbour
SW115	Worting Junction to Exeter St Davids
SW120	Pirbright Junction to Alton
SW125	Southcote Junction to Basingstoke
SW130	Eastleigh to Romsey
SW135	Eastleigh to Fareham
SW140	St Denys to Portcreek Junction
SW145	Northam Junction to Canute Road
SW147	Southampton to Southampton Western Docks

SW150	Redbridge to Salisbury Tunnel Junction
SW155	Totton to Fawley (Goods Line)
SW160	Brockenhurst to Lymington Pier
SW165	Hamworthy to Hamworthy Goods (Goods Line)
SW166	Worgret Junction to Furzebrook
SW170	Westbury South Junction (excl) to Wilton Junction
SW175	Castle Cary Junction to Dorchester Junction
SW180	Raynes Park to Horsham
SW185	Motspur Park to Chessington South
SW190	New Malden to Shepperton
SW195	Hampton Court Junction to Hampton Court
SW200	Hampton Court Junction to Guildford (via Cobham)
SW205	Leatherhead to Effingham Junction
SW210	Clapham Junction to Southcote Junction (via Reading)
SW220	Latchmere Junction to Kensington Olympia
SW225	Point Pleasant Junction to Wimbledon
SW230	Barnes to Feltham Junction (via Hounslow)
SW240	Kew East Jn to Old Kew Jn
SW245	Twickenham to Shacklegate Junction
SW250	Staines to Windsor and Eton Riverside
SW255	Virginia Water to Weybridge
SW260	Ascot to Ash Vale Junction
SW265	Guildford to Wokingham
SW300	Gomshall to Shalford Junction

Other codes which appear in all or in part in this book

EA1310	Camden Road West Jn to Richmond
EA1320	Camden Road West Jn to Stratford Platforms 1 and 2
EA1325	Highbury And Islington to New Cross/New Cross Gate
EA1327	Silwood Jn to Old Kent Road Jn
EA1330	South Acton Jn to Old Kew Jn & New Kew Jn
MD160	Willesden High Level Jn to Mitre Bridge Jn
MD166	North Pole Junction to Wembley
GW103	Paddington to Uffington
GW108	Fordgate to Penzance
GW110	Old Oak Common West to South Ruislip (excl)
GW130	Acton Wells Jn (excl) to Acton East Jn
GW190	Reading Spur Jn to Reading New Jn
GW195	Reading Southern Jn to Reading East Jn (Reading Low Level Lines)
GW220	Reading Oxford Road Jn to Reading West Jn
GW225	Reading Caversham Road Jn to Oxford Road Jn (Reading Feeder Lines)
GW500	Reading (Westbury Line Jn) to Cogload Jn via (Westbury and Frome Avoiding Lines)
GW606	Crannaford Level Crossing (incl.) to Exeter St. Davids.
GW610	Cowley Bridge Jn to Barnstaple
XR001	Westbourne Park Jn to Pudding Mill Lane Boundary
XR002	Stepney Green Jn to Alsike Road Jn
LN110	Canonbury West Jn to Finsbury Park
LN3201	St Pancras to Tapton Jn (via Derby)
LN3213	Farringdon to Kentish Town

Engineer's Line References

This listing is intended to show all the relevant operational ELRs that appear in this book, those that were live in the last edition but now closed, out of use or lifted and those that have carried over from the original network onto Heritage lines. More information can be found about these codes on the excellent website by Phil Deaves (see Bibliography). The location of the start and finish boundary of each ELR can be found in the book from the map reference in the Location Index applicable to any of the locations named in the description. Some ELRs extend over several pages.

AAV	Ascot Jn - Ash Vale Jn
ACR	Ashford - Ramsgate (via Canterbury West)
ACW	Acton Canal Wharf - Willesden
AGE	Swanage Branch (Heritage)
AGW	Angerstein Wharf Branch
AHG	Nine Elms Jn - Linford Street Jn
AIW	Alton, Itchen Abbas and Winchester Line (Heritage)
AJB	Addlestone Jn - Byfleet Jn
ANL	Acton and Northolt Line: Old Oak Common West Jn - Northolt Jn
APL	Appledore - Lydd Town (Goods Line)
ATG	Turnham Green (LU Bdy) - Gunnersbury Jn
ATH	Ashford 'D' Jn - Hastings
ATL	Battersea Park Jn - Peckham Rye (Atlantic Line/South London Line)
AWL	Acton Wells Line: Acton East - Acton Wells Jn
BAA	Basingstoke - Alton Butts Jn (siding)
BAE	Basingstoke (Worting Jn) - Exeter St Davids
BBD9	Bournemouth West Carriage Sidings
BBJ	Balham Jn - Beckenham Jn
BBR	Barnham Jn - Bognor Regis
BDH	Brent Curve Jn - Dudding Hill Jn
BEX	St. Johns Jn - Crayford Creek Jn via Bexleyheath
BHL	Berks and Hants line (Southcote Jn - Patney & Chirton Jn)
BJN	Bromley Jn - Norwood Jn
BKE	Basingstoke Branch (Reading Westbury line Jn - Basingstoke)
BLI	Brighton (West Coast) - Littlehampton
BLP	Brockenhurst - Lymington Pier
BME	Buckland Jn - Minster East Jn
BMJ	Blackfriars Jn - Metropolitan Jn
BML	Waterloo (Main lines) - Weymouth (Bournemouth Main line)
BNG	Bromley North - Grove Park Jn
BOK	Broad Street and Old Kew Line via Hampstead (North London Line)
BPJ	Lovers Walk Depot
BPW	Botley - Bishops Waltham
BRB	Brentford Branch
BSF	Battersea Pier Jn (LCD) - Stewarts Lane - Factory Jn
BSP	Battersea Pier Jn (LBSC) - Stewarts Lane - Longhedge Jn - Pouparts Jn
BTC	Blackheath Jn - Charlton Jn
BTE	Barking: Tilbury line Jn East - Barking East Jn
BTH	South Bermondsey Jn - Horsham
BTL	Brighton (East Coast) - Lewes Jn
BWT	Barking W. Jn - Barking Tilbury line Jn West
CAT	Brixton Jn - Shortlands Jn (Catford Loop)
CAW	Cricklewood Curve Jn - Acton Wells Jn
CBM	Cannon Street - Borough Market Jn
CCL	Castle Cary and Langport: Castle Cary - Cogload
CFP	Canonbury - Finsbury Park Curve
CJA	Copyhold Jn - Ardingly
CJL	Clapham Junction (Ludgate Jn) - Latchmere No.2 Jn
CKL	Longhedge Jn (Calvert Rd Jn) - Latchmere No.1 Jn
CLA	Ashford, Chart Leacon Depot
CLJ	Clapham Junction Sidings
CMJ	West Croydon - Mitcham Jn (now London Trams)
CNS	Carpenters Road North Jn - South Jn
CRA	Crayford Spur 'B' Jn - Crayford Spur 'A' Jn
CSM	Chislehurst Jn - St. Mary Cray Jn (Chatham Loops)
CSW	Metropolitan Jn - Cannon Street South Jn
CWJ	Camden Jn - Watford Jn (DC Electric lines)

CYD	Chatham Dockyard Branch (lifted)
DAC	Devon & Cornwall: Cowley Bridge Jn - Meldon
DRN	Waterloo and City Line ('The Drain' - London Underground)
DWW	Dalston Jn - Navarino Road
ECM	East Coast Main Line, London, Kings Cross - Edinburgh
ECR	Eastleigh East Jn (Chandler's Ford) - Romsey Jn
EKR	Shepherdswell Jn - Tilmanstone Colliery (EKLR) (Heritage)
ELL	East London Line
EMT	Exeter and Exmouth Line
EPP	Epping Branch
ETF	Eastleigh West Jn - Fareham East Jn
EYD	Eastleigh Yards
FDM	Faversham - Dover Priory
FFH	Folkestone East Jn - Folkestone Harbour
FJJ	Farlington Jn - Cosham Jn
FJL	Ford Jn - Littlehampton Jn
FJS	Fawkham Jn - Southfleet Jn
FLL	Factory Jn - Longhedge Jn - Lavender Hill Jn - Clapham Jn (Ludgate Jn)
FSS	Fenchurch Street - Shoeburyness
FTB	Fareham West Jn - Bedenham Sidings (Closed)
FTL	Farringdon Jn - (Ludgate) Blackfriars
FUR	Worgret Jn - Furzebrook Sidings
GEC	Greenford East Curve
GFB	Gas Factory Jn - Bow Jn
GJB	Grove Junction - Birchden Junction (Heritage)
GTW	Guildford North Jn - Wokingham Jn
HAG	Hamworthy Goods Branch
HAM	Hampton Court Branch
HDR	Hither Green Jn, Dartford and Rochester Line
HGG1	Hurst Green Jn - East Grinstead
HGG2	Culver Jn - East Grinstead (Heritage)
HGP	Hither Green/Grove Park Sidings
HHH	(Holborn Viaduct) Blackfriars - Herne Hill South Jn
HHT	Herne Hill South Jn - Tulse Hill South Jn
HJW	Hounslow Jn - Whitton Jn
HOU	Barnes Jn - Hounslow - Feltham Jn (Hounslow Loop)
HSE	Hawkesbury Street Jn - Archcliffe Jn
HTG	Hoo Jn - Grain (Goods Line)
IOW	Ryde Pier Head - Shanklin (Isle of Wight)
IWM	Isle of Wight, Merstone - Sandown Branch (Sandown Sdgs)
KJE	Keymer Jn - Eastbourne
KSU	Kent and East Sussex Railway (Heritage)
LAV	Laverstock North Jn - Laverstock South Jn - 'Laverstock Loop'
LBC	London Bridge (Platforms 14-16) - Bricklayers Arms Jn (South London Spur line)
LBW	London Bridge (Platforms 8-13) - Windmill Bridge Jn
LCH	Lewisham East Jn (Ladywell line) - Hayes
LEE	Lee Jn - Lee Spur Jn
LEJ	Leatherhead Jn - Effingham Jn
LLL	Parks Bridge Jn - Ladywell Jn (Ladywell Loop)
LOC	Loughborough Jn - Canterbury Road Jn
LTC	Loughborough Jn - Cambria Jn
LTH	Leigham Jn - Tulse Hill Jn (Leigham Spur)

LTN	London, Liverpool St. - Norwich via Ipswich
LUD	Andover - Ludgershall
LVT	Lewisham Vale Jn - Tanners Hill Jn
MCL	Kentish Town Jn - Moorgate (Midland City line)
MIS	Millbrook - Southampton Western Docks
MJW	Mitcham Jn - Wimbledon (now London Trams)
MLN	Main Line, Paddington - Penzance (via Bristol T.M.)
MOD	MOD Chilmark Branch (closed)
MPC	Motspur Park - Chessington South
MSW	Minster South Jn - Minster West Jn
NAJ	Neasden South Jn - Aynho Jn
NBB	New Beckenham Jn - Beckenham Jn
NCS	Courthill Loop Jn North - Courthill Loop Jn South (Courthill Loop)
NFE	Norwood Jn (Wallington Line Jn) - Epsom Downs
NGL	Hampton Court Jn - Guildford, New Line Jn (New Guildford Line)
NHB	Newhaven Harbour Jn - Newhaven Harbour
NKE	New Kew Jn - Kew East Jn
NKL	North Kent East Jn - Dartford (via Greenwich)
NLI	North London Incline
NMS	New Malden Jn - Shepperton
NSA	Aldershot South Jn - Aldershot North Jn
NTL	Nunhead Jn - Lewisham Jn
NYD	Norwood Yard and Selhurst Workshop Sidings
OJS	Otford Jn - Sevenoaks Jn
PAA	Pirbright Jn - Alton
PAS	Portsmouth, Blackfriars Jn - Portsmouth & Southsea Low level
PAT	Purley - Caterham
PBE	Putney Bridge - East Putney Jn
PPH	Preston Park - Hove
PPW	Point Pleasant Jn - Wimbledon (LU platforms)
PSF	Perry Street Fork Jn - Slade Green Jn
PWS	Paddock Wood - Strood (via Maidstone West)
QRT1	Queen's Park Depot Through Lines (Road 24)
QRT2	Queen's Park Depot Through Lines (Road 21)
RDG	Waterloo (Windsor lines) - Reading
RED	Stoats Nest Jn - Redhill - Earlswood Jn (Redhill line)
REY	Ramsgate East Yards
RFR	Reading Feeder Lines
RLL	Reading Low Level Lines
RNJ	Reading Spur Jn - Reading New Jn
RNS	Ramsgate New Sidings
ROU	Romford - Upminster
RPE	Raynes Park Jn - Epsom Jn
RSJ	Redhill, Guildford Line Jn - Shalford Jn
RTR1	Reading Triangle DMU Sidings
RTJ	Redbridge Jn - Salisbury, Tunnel Jn
RTT	Redhill, Tonbridge Line Jn - Tonbridge West Jn
RVC	Ravensbourne Chord
RWC	Reading West Curve
SAL	Westbury South Jn - Wilton Jn (Salisbury Branch)
SAR	South Acton Jn - Richmond
SBJ	Swanley - Ashford
SCC	West London Jn - Latchmere No.3 Jn (Sheepcote Curve)

SCP	Sydenham Jn - Crystal Palace, Tunnel Jn
SCU1	South Croydon Jn - Uckfield
SCU2	Lewes - Uckfield (Heritage)
SDP	St. Denys Jn - Portcreek Jn
SEJ	Sittingbourne (Eastern Jn) - Sheerness-on-Sea
SEV	Sevington Sidings
SHF	Strawberry Hill Jn - Fulwell Jn
SLC	Stewarts Lane Sidings
SLJ	Slow Lines Junctions (Streatham North - South Junctions)
SMS	Streatham South Jn - Sutton (via Wimbledon)
SNS	Streatham North Jn (Fast line) - Streatham South Jn (Fast line)
SOY	Northam Jn - Southampton Eastern Docks
SPC	St. Pancras - Chesterfield (Midland Main Line)
SSC	Streatham Jn - Streatham Common Jn
STS	Southerham Jn - Seaford
SWE	Staines Jn - Windsor & Eton Riverside
SWX	Staines West Link Line (closed)
TAH	Tottenham and Hampstead
TAT	Chipstead Line Jn (Purley - Tattenham Corner
TBH	Three Bridges Jn - Havant Jn via Horsham
TLL	Tilbury Loop Line
TLP	Bickley Jn - Petts Wood Jn (Tonbridge Loops)
TML	Saltwood Jn/Continental Jn - Eurotunnel boundary (Trans-Manche Link)
TRL	St.Pancras - Eurotunnel Interface (HS1)
TSJ	Twickenham Jn - Shacklegate Jn
TTF	Totton - Fawley
TTH	Tonbridge - Bo Peep Jn
UPG	Upminster - Grays
VIR	Victoria - Ramsgate (via Herne Hill and Chatham)
VTB	Victoria (Central) - Brighton via Streatham Common and Quarry line
VWW	Virginia Water - Weybridge
WAW	Willesden, Low level Goods Jn - Acton Wells Jn
WCS	Selhurst Jn - Gloucester Road Jn
WEL	West Ealing Loop: West Ealing - Greenford
WEY	(Weymouth line): Thingley Jn - Dorchester Jn
WJB	Willingden Jn - Bopeep Jn
WKG	Woking Yards
WLL	Clapham Junction, Falcon Jn - Willesden, West London Jn (West London Line)
WLL9	Former North Pole Channel Tunnel Carriage Servicing Depot (now Hitachi)
WMB	Willesden High Level Jn - Mitre Bridge Jn
WMS	Sittingbourne Western Jn - Middle Jn
WPH	Woking Jn - Portsmouth Harbour (Portsmouth Direct line)
WPK	Wimbledon Park and Depot Sidings
WTH	West Norwood Jn - Tulse Hill Jn (West Norwood Spur)
WTQ	Weymouth Jn - Weymouth Quay (closed)
XRC	Westbourne Park Jn - Stepney Green Jn
XRNE	Stepney Green Jn - Pudding Mill Lane boundary
XRSE	Stepney Green Jn - Alsike Road Jn
XTD	Charing Cross/Cannon Street - Dover Priory/Eurotunnel Interface (via Tonbridge)
YJP	Yeovil Pen Mill Jn - Yeovil Jn

Bibliography

The Publisher is grateful for the access given by Network Rail to a significant range of internal documents, most particularly the Sectional Appendix, Weekly and Periodic Operating Notices, Signalling Notices and Isolation Diagrams. In addition, a large number of other references have been used, the most reliable of which are:

Railway Passenger Stations in Great Britain – A Chronology (4th Edition)
By Michael Quick, Railway & Canal Historical Society, Oxford OX2 0NP

Signalling Atlas and Signal Box Directory (3rd Edition)
By Peter Kay and David Allen, Signalling Record Society, Wallasey, CH45 4PZ

The Railway Data Series (20 volumes covering the British Isles, mile by mile)
By Michael Oakley, Sword Press, Sutton Coldfield, B73 5UL

The Railways of Great Britain – A Historical Atlas (3rd Edition)
By Colonel Michael H. Cobb, Patrick S. Cobb, Newbury, RG20 9LB

Minor Railways in the British Isles series (4 volumes of track plans)
By Peter Scott, Published by P Scott, Reading RG30 2DQ

Branch Line News
Published fortnightly by the Branch Line Society, Bristol BS34 8NP

The 'Signalling Digest' compiled by Andrew Overton
Published bi-monthly by Signalling Record Society

Island Line
By Ralph C. Humphries, Coach House Publications Ltd, East Cowes, PO32 6QQ

Gradients of the British Main Line Railways
Crecy Publishing Ltd, Manchester, M22 5LH

The 'Trackwatch' column from Modern Railways Magazine
2004-2011, by the late Gerald Jacobs
2011-2014, by Mike Bridge
2015 onwards, by Martyn Brailsford

British Rail National Route Codes; Catalogue of Route Sections at 1st January 1973
British Rail National Route Code Catalogue: List of Route Sections at 1st April 1986

Websites:
http://www.railwaycodes.org.uk, a site by Phil Deaves which details ELRs, past and present, LORs, Signal Box codes and a host of other useful information
http://www.railscot.co.uk, Ewan Crawford's wide-ranging site and a source of much visual information.
http://maps.nls.uk, the National Library of Scotland which includes UK-wide old OS mapping at different scales
http://www.old-maps.co.uk, another source of old OS mapping
http://www.disused-stations.org.uk, a source of information about station histories
https://www.whatdotheyknow.com, a site collecting the results of FOI requests
https://www.google.co.uk/maps and Google Earth, site and software providing aerial photography, often at a range of dates and over which detailed distance measurement can be made.

Chains to Yards to Km Conversion Table

80 chains = 1 mile = 1.609 Km

Chains	Yards	Km equivalent	Chains	Yards	Km equivalent	Chains	Yards	Km equivalent
1	22	0.020	28	616	0.563	55	1,210	1.106
2	44	0.040	29	638	0.583	56	1,232	1.127
3	66	0.060	30	660	0.604	57	1,254	1.147
4	88	0.080	31	682	0.624	58	1,276	1.167
5	110	0.101	32	704	0.644	59	1,298	1.187
6	132	0.121	33	726	0.664	60	1,320	1.207
7	154	0.141	34	748	0.684	61	1,342	1.227
8	176	0.161	35	770	0.704	62	1,364	1.247
9	198	0.181	36	792	0.724	63	1,386	1.267
10	220	0.201	37	814	0.744	64	1,408	1.287
11	242	0.221	38	836	0.764	65	1,430	1.308
12	264	0.241	39	858	0.785	66	1,452	1.328
13	286	0.262	40	880	0.805	67	1,474	1.348
14	308	0.282	41	902	0.825	68	1,496	1.368
15	330	0.302	42	924	0.845	69	1,518	1.388
16	352	0.322	43	946	0.865	70	1,540	1.408
17	374	0.342	44	968	0.885	71	1,562	1.428
18	396	0.362	45	990	0.905	72	1,584	1.448
19	418	0.382	46	1,012	0.925	73	1,606	1.469
20	440	0.402	47	1,034	0.945	74	1,628	1.489
21	462	0.422	48	1,056	0.966	75	1,650	1.509
22	484	0.443	49	1,078	0.986	76	1,672	1.529
23	506	0.463	50	1,100	1.006	77	1,694	1.549
24	528	0.483	51	1,122	1.026	78	1,716	1.569
25	550	0.503	52	1,144	1.046	79	1,738	1.589
26	572	0.523	53	1,166	1.066	80	1,760	1.609
27	594	0.543	54	1,188	1.086			